The
New Zealand Blouse

By Martha Campbell Pullen, Ph. D.

May God Bless You

Martha Pullen

Book Team

Book Design and Layout
Kelly Chambers

Contributing Sewing Designers
Beverley Sheldrick and Sue Pennington

Construction Consultants
Kathy McMakin, Charlotte Potter, Patty Smith,
Louise Baird, Meredith Miller and Diane Bradshaw

Illustrated By
Kris Broom and Angela Pullen

Photography
Jennifer & Company

Printed By
Lithographics, Inc.
Nashville, TN

Published and Distributed By
Martha Pullen Company, Inc.
518 Madison Street
Huntsville, Alabama 35801-4286
Phone 256-533-9586
Fax 256-533-9630

Library of Congress Catalog Card Number 99-70132

ISBN 1-878048-20-1

This book is dedicated to Beverley Sheldrick and her family, Kenneth, Christopher and Vanessa.

It gives me great pleasure to dedicate this book to Beverley Sheldrick because it was she who designed the original New Zealand blouse and who made several of the blouses. What a joy it was for me to meet Beverley Sheldrick on my first trip to Australia teaching for Gloria McKinnon at Anne's Glory Box in New Castle, New South Wales. She was already an advanced embroiderer and perfection seamstress so sharing heirloom techniques with her was very easy. Since she and Lynne Holyoake both won the design contest, she came again the next year. She laughingly calls herself a "slow learner" because she kept telling her husband, Kenneth, that she had to come over and over again to Martha's schools because she just couldn't get it.

Beverley makes the most wonderful tailored heirloom blouses with absolutely enchanting embroidery on each. Even with lace and embroidery her blouses still seem tailored and very wearable. Beverley began designing blouses for *Sew Beautiful* magazine as well as other beautiful garments and embroidery designs. I invited her to travel to Tuscaloosa to teach silk ribbon embroidery on our television series; the rest is history.

Beverley started sewing at the age of five, making all of her doll's clothes. Her mother bought her a tiny toy sewing machine, which was not a success, and she moved to her mother's old treadle machine. She made her first garment for herself at the age of eight, and it wasn't long before she was making all her own clothes.She had discovered that if she did this, her father would always give her the money for some new fabric. It was a great way to get new clothes!

She learned at a very early age, when her mother was proudly showing her latest doll's creation to a friend, that the inside had to be as beautiful as the outside. Beverley was horrified even at the age of five when her mother turned it inside out and said "But you haven't done a very good job on the inside." Little did she know that this would have a tremendous influence in her later life.

At school, she learned sewing and cooking, and she would have dearly loved to have become a home economics teacher. Unfortunately the only home economics training college was at the other end of the country, and her family could not afford to send her there. Her mother believed that if she took a business course she would always be able to earn a living, and her mother was quite right.

At the age of eighteen, Beverley started traveling and went to Australia where she spent a year.She then went home for a month to meet her baby sister, who was by this time six months old; Beverley wasn't to see her again for five years, for she was on her way to England to work. On the trip to England, she met her husband; it was a shipboard romance that was to last, and they were married in England two years later in a tiny, 13th century country church.Her first job was with a family as nanny to their two small boys, and it was in their home that she was married; Paul, the father, gave her away. She and Kenneth were to become lifetime friends with this family. After she was married, she and Kenneth lived in London and spent all of their spare time either in a museum or at an art gallery, and at night, it would be the theater or a concert or the ballet. They traveled as much as they possibly could when money would allow. After five years, they went home to Australia to care for Kenneth's father. They had two children, Christopher and Vanessa. Eight years later, they moved to New Zealand and started a business as antique dealers.

She had always loved the beautiful clothes that the actresses wore in the plays she attended, and she fancied herself swanning around in a glorious peignoir. Beverley loved the beautiful garments in Adrien and at Misses Bonney, a shop in Sydney, and would stand like a child outside a sweetie shop just drooling over them.

Beverley writes, "I couldn't afford to buy them, so I was delighted some years later when I was living in New Zealand to have a conversation with an Australian girl and to find there was a shop teaching this beautiful heirloom sewing. The class took four weeks, one day a week. I couldn't afford to go for a month, but I had a friend who was moving to Australia and would, coincidentally, live close by this shop. I persuaded this friend to go and take the class with my promise that if she would come back and teach us all, I would arrange enough people to make it possible; and that was the start of it all! When I look back, what she taught us was very basic, and I had to teach myself a lot from books. Quite by accident, I was visiting a shop in Auckland to get some doll's buttons for Nanny (Miss Elizabeth), and, in conversation with the owner, was persuaded to join a class in silk ribbon with Gloria McKinnon. I didn't have a clue what I was going to learn, but it seemed like a good idea. Not only did I just love the class, but she also told me about the wonderful Martha Pullen School she was going to have in Newcastle; so, another of the turning points in my life was about to start. I loved the school, and I was just in seventh heaven; I had Martha, Margaret Boyles and Kathy McMakin as instructors. I realized all the things I wasn't doing correctly, and the following year Lynne Holyoake and I were joint first-prize winners of the competition, and we were to become great friends. The prize, of course, was free entry to next year's school; so once more I was crossing the Tasman Sea. I was to continue to do this for the following five years; I guess Martha would say I was a 'real slow learner'! But I had come to love the things we did, the people I met, and the friends I had made."

"The last time, Martha said, 'Beverley, I think you've been coming as a student long enough; I think it's time you came and taught at my school in America.' I had, of course, in this period, had one trip to Huntsville as a student, so I was thrilled to be invited to teach. The following year it was an enormous thrill to be invited to appear on Martha's television program, *Martha's Sewing Room*, and I have just finished the third year's programs; little did I know when I worked for Southern Television in England on the selling side that one day I would be on the other side of television."

"I have been teaching a wide range of subjects in New Zealand for perhaps ten years now, and I have tried to use the wonderful techniques in quilts, adult clothing and many other ways. Many students have said 'But I wouldn't wear lace!' But when they see me in my tailored blouses with lace insertion and pintucks, they realize that lace is not only for little girls; why should they have all the fun!"

"I have always had a deeply religious background. As a small girl, I lived on a farm at the top of a valley. We had no churches, but we had a wonderful man who, every Sunday, would bring his car to the top of the valley, collect all the children and take them to an non-denominational Sunday school. This was all done at his expense, and we were never asked for a collection or a donation; he was truly a Christian man. We sang wonderful songs, and he would accompany us on a banjo or a ukulele; there were lots of action songs and fun. We would then have half an hour in small groups, reading and learning the Bible. When my parents moved into town, my family joined St. Andrew's Anglican Church, which is housed in a very beautiful historic wooden building. It is my very great privilege today to be a member of the Linen Guild, the Vestry Guild, and to be both a reader and a server in this church I have loved for most of my life. In retrospect, I can see God's hand in the way I have been prepared to do the things I do now; my wish to be a teacher in sewing has been fulfilled."

"Martha Pullen has done much to change my life. I would like to thank her for her love, her guidance and encouragement, and for the many opportunities she has given me. May God bless her and continue to use her in the wonderful way He does."

Beverley has written a book, *Colonial Inspirations*, has had work published in *Fancywork*, *Sew Beautiful*, *Inspirations* and *Anne's Glory Box*. She still teaches in New Zealand and has several books in the making, but is very busy working, designing, and teaching for Martha Pullen! Beverley would want me to tell you that although she designed the blouse and made several of the blouses, Sue Pennington made most of the versions of her blouse for the televison show and for this series. We also thank Sue Pennington for her "re-creations" of Beverley's blouse.

Table of Contents

General Blouse Directions

Fabric Requirements

All sizes: 45" wide fabric
$2^7/8$ yards for blouse with short sleeves
$3^1/3$ yards for blouse with 3/4 sleeves
$3^1/2$ yards for blouse with long sleeves

The above yardage is for a plain blouse with yoke. It does not include extra fabric for linings, collar, tucks or embellished pieces. Refer to the specific directions for the measurement for each blouse.

Notions: $1/8$ yard interfacing for cuffs (optional), six $1/2$" buttons for the back, 2 buttons for the cuff

Lace and Trims Requirement - Refer to specific directions under each blouse title.

All pattern pieces are found on the pattern pull-out. The measurements for the cuffs are found on the Cuff Chart in Section III. All templates are found on the pattern pull-out unless otherwise indicated.

All seams are $1/4$" unless otherwise noted. Overcast the seam allowances using a zigzag or serger. French seams can be used, if desired. When tracing a design or pattern piece, use a wash-out marker or pencil.

Very Important: Read both the general directions and the specific directions before cutting or sewing the blouse desired. The general directions list options for neck finishes, sleeve finishes, general construction techniques, yoke options and finishing details. The specific directions list the stitching order and any additional directions needed to complete the specific blouse.

I. Sizing

The ladies blouses are sized as follows:
XS = 6 - 8   L = 18 - 20   S = 10 - 12
XL = 22 - 24   M = 14 - 16   XXL = 26 - 28

II. Neck Finishes

A. Entredeux to Gathered Edging Lace

1. Sew shoulder seams of yoke with a $1/4$" seam (fig. 1). **NOTE:** The shoulder seams may have already been sewn if embellishment was done.
2. Measure around the neck edge with the back facing extended and add 1 inch. Cut a strip of entredeux to this length.
3. Cut a piece of edging lace twice as long as the entredeux. Gather the edging lace to fit the entredeux strip.
4. Trim away one side of the entredeux fabric (fig. 2) and attach the gathered edging lace to the trimmed entredeux using the technique "gathered lace to entredeux".

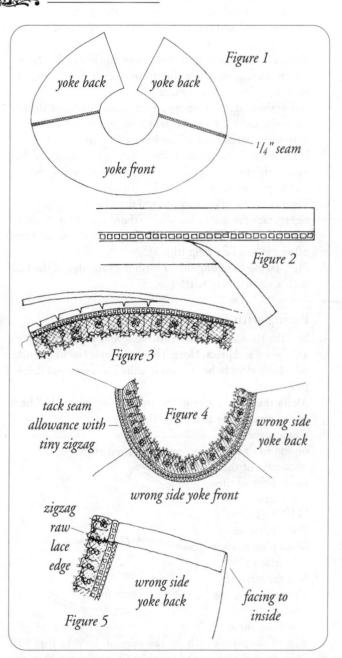

Figure 1

yoke back   yoke back

$1/4$" seam

yoke front

Figure 2

Figure 3

Figure 4

tack seam allowance with tiny zigzag

wrong side yoke back

wrong side yoke front

zigzag raw lace edge

wrong side yoke back

facing to inside

Figure 5

5. If the fabric edge remaining on the entredeux is not already $1/4$", trim to $1/4$". Clip this fabric so that it will curve around the neck of the yoke (fig. 3).
6. Place this strip and the yoke (back facing extended) of the blouse, right sides together. Attach neck band using the technique "entredeux to fabric" (fig. 4).
7. Press the seam allowance toward the blouse. Using a tiny zigzag, tack the seam allowance to the blouse. This stitching will keep the entredeux/gathered lace standing up at the neck. Trim off the excess lace strip (fig. 4).
8. Press facing to wrong side. Finish the raw edge of the lace with a small zigzag stitch (fig. 5).

B. Entredeux to Flat Lace

1. Place the front yoke to the back yokes and stitch together at the shoulders (see fig. 1).
2. Measure around the neck edge with the back facing extended and add one inch. Cut a strip of entredeux and lace edging to this length.
3. Trim away one side of the entredeux fabric (see fig. 2) and attach the edging lace to the trimmed entredeux using the technique "entredeux to lace".
4. If the fabric edge remaining on the entredeux is not already ¹/₄", trim to ¹/₄". Clip this fabric so that it will curve around the neck edge of the blouse (fig. 6).
5. Place the strip to the neck (back facing extended) of the blouse right sides together. Attach the strip using the technique "entredeux to fabric" (fig. 7).
6. Press the seam allowance toward the blouse. Using a tiny zigzag, tack the seam allowance to the blouse. This stitching will keep the entredeux/lace standing up at the neck. Trim off the excess lace strip (fig. 7).
7. Press facing to wrong side. Finish the raw edge of the lace with a small zigzag stitch (fig. 8).

C. Piping with Facing

1. Sew the shoulder seams of the yoke and yoke lining with a ¹/₄" seam and press. Note: The shoulder seams of the yoke may have already been sewn if embellishment was done (see fig. 1).
2. Along the lower curve of the yoke lining, turn a ¹/₄" hem to the wrong side and press (fig. 9).
3. Cut a piece of piping to fit the neck edge of the yoke (refer to the technique "Making Piping"). If the fabric edge of the piping is not ¹/₄", trim to ¹/₄". Sew the strip of piping around the edge of the yoke matching the raw edge of the piping with the raw edge of the yoke (fig. 10).
4. Place the yoke lining and the yoke right sides together, the piping will be sandwiched between the yokes, and stitch the neck seam with a ¹/₄" seam (fig. 11).
5. Trim to an ¹/₈" if necessary and clip the neck seam around the curve (fig. 11).
6. Turn the lining to the inside and press well (fig. 12).

D. Scalloped Bias

1. Cut strips of bias that are 1¹/₂" wide. Strips may be seamed together as for piping to have a strip the length needed.

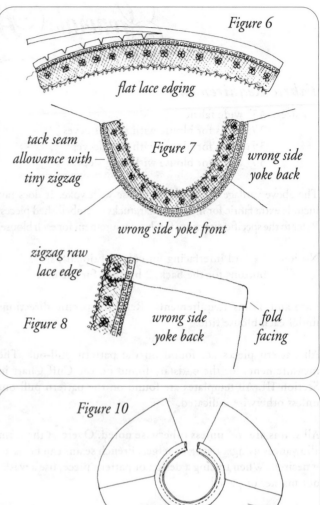

Figure 6

flat lace edging

tack seam allowance with tiny zigzag

Figure 7

wrong side yoke back

wrong side yoke front

zigzag raw lace edge

Figure 8

wrong side yoke back

fold facing

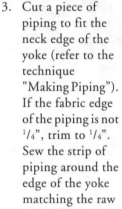
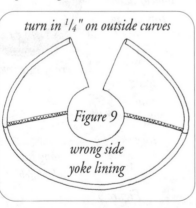

turn in ¹/₄" on outside curves

Figure 9

wrong side yoke lining

Figure 10

stitch piping to neck edge

yoke

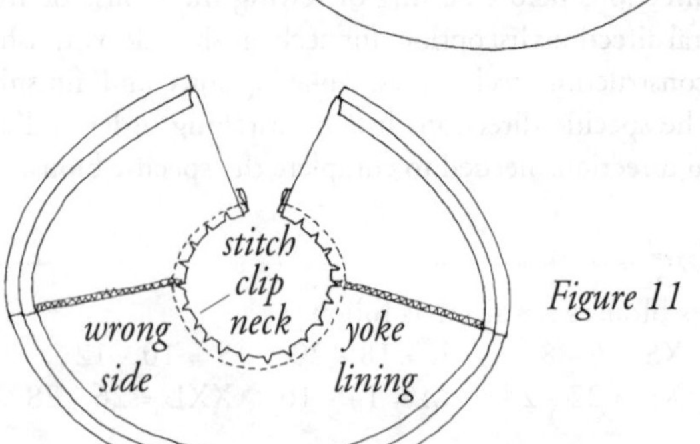

stitch clip neck

wrong side

yoke lining

Figure 11

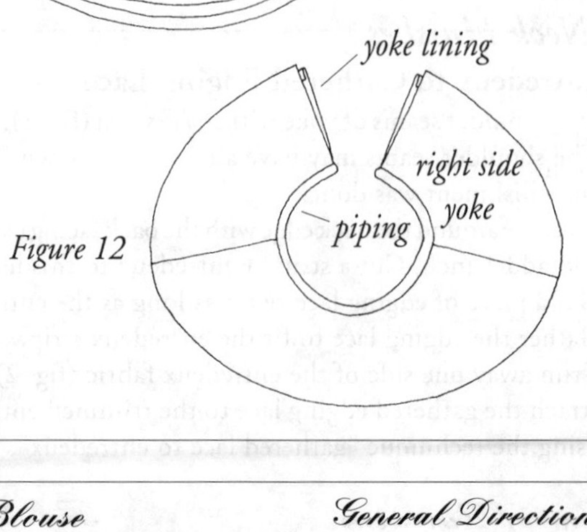

yoke lining

right side yoke

Figure 12

piping

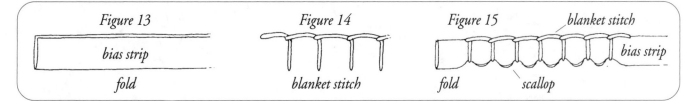

Figure 13   bias strip   fold

Figure 14   blanket stitch

Figure 15   blanket stitch   bias strip   fold   scallop

2. Fold the bias in half and press(fig. 13).
3. Choose a stitch on your machine similar to a blanket stitch (fig. 14).
4. Stitch along the bias so that the needle swings off the folded edge when stitching (fig. 15).
5. Tighten the tension on your machine to cause the stitch to "pull" creating the scallop.
6. This strip can be used in place of piping.

E. Collar

1. Place the yoke front and yoke backs right sides together and stitch the shoulder seams with a $^1/_4$" seam (see fig. 1).
2. Place the wrong side of the collar to the right side of the neck of the yoke. Pin in place. Fold the yoke back facing on the fold line to the right side of the yoke (collar will be between yoke back and facing) (fig. 16).
3. Cut a bias strip 1" wide by 23". Fold the bias strip in half and press. Place the cut edges of the strip to the neck of the collar/yoke. Bias strip starts and stops $^1/_2$" from the back edge. Cut off any excess bias (fig. 17).
4. Stitch the bias strip to the neck edge using a $^1/_4$" seam, starting at the fold lines on the back edges of the yoke (fig. 17).
5. Trim the seam to $^1/_8$". Clip the neck edge and understitch the bias band. Understitching is done by stitching through the bias band and the trimmed seams (fig. 18).
6. Flip the bias strip and the back bodice facings to the inside of the yoke. Hand stitch the bias strip in place finishing the neck edge, or stitch the band down on the sewing machine about $^1/_4$" from the neck edge. Start at the back edge and go all the way around the neck. The collar will be pulled up so that the stitching does not go through the collar (fig. 19).

F. Lined Yoke

1. Sew the shoulder seams of the yoke and yoke lining with a $^1/_4$" seam and press (see fig. 1). Note: The shoulder seams of the yoke may have already been sewn if embellishment was done.
2. Along the lower curve of the yoke lining, turn a $^1/_4$" hem to the wrong side and press (see fig. 9).
3. Place the yoke lining and the yoke right sides together matching the shoulder seams, and stitch the neck seam with a $^1/_4$" seam (fig. 20).
4. Trim to $^1/_8$" and clip the neck seam around the curve (fig. 20).
5. Turn the lining to the inside and press well (fig. 21).

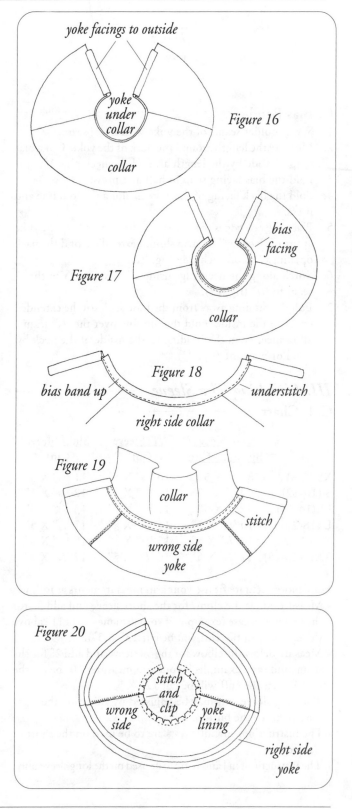

yoke facings to outside

yoke under collar

collar

Figure 16

Figure 17

bias facing

collar

Figure 18

bias band up   understitch

right side collar

Figure 19

collar

stitch

wrong side yoke

Figure 20

stitch and clip

wrong side   yoke lining

right side yoke

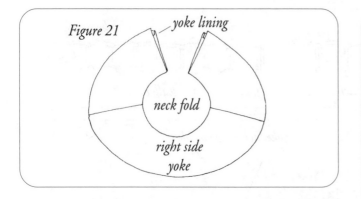

Figure 21

yoke lining

neck fold

right side
yoke

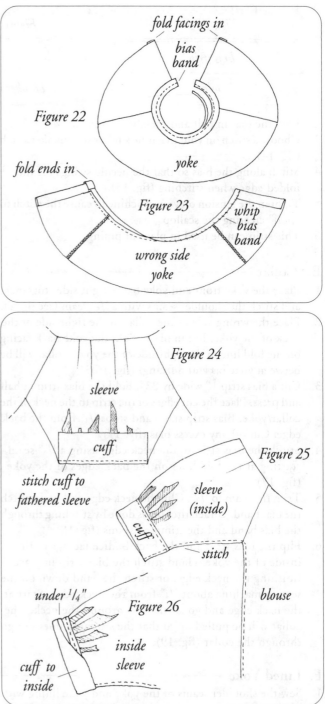

fold facings in

bias band

Figure 22

yoke

fold ends in

Figure 23

whip bias band

wrong side yoke

Figure 24

sleeve

cuff

stitch cuff to fathered sleeve

Figure 25

sleeve (inside)

cuff

stitch

blouse

under 1/4"

Figure 26

inside sleeve

cuff to inside

G. Bias Band

1. Sew shoulder seams of the yoke with a $^1/_4$" seam.
2. Measure the length around the neck of the yoke. Cut a bias strip 2" wide by the length around the neck plus 1".
3. Fold the bias facing strip in half and press.
4. Fold the back facing of the yoke in along the fold line and press.
5. Place the raw edges of the strip to the right side of the yoke at the neck edge. The strip should extend beyond the back openings $^1/_2$" on each side (fig. 22).
6. Stitch along the neck edge using a $^1/_2$" seam. Trim the seam to $^1/_4$" (fig. 22).
7. Pull the binding away from the blouse. Turn the extended edges to the inside. Fold the binding over the $^1/_4$" seam allowance. Hem the binding to the inside of the neck by hand or machine (fig. 23).

III. Finishing The Sleeve
Cuff Chart

	Long Sleeve Buttoned Cuff	$^3/_4$" Sleeve Cuff	Short Sleeve Cuff
XS (6-8)	8 $^7/_8$" X 5"	10 $^3/_4$" X 5"	11 $^3/_4$" X 5"
S (10-12)	9 $^1/_4$" X 5"	10 $^3/_4$" X 5"	12 $^3/_4$" X 5"
M (14-16)	9 $^3/_4$" X 5"	11 $^1/_4$" X 5"	13 $^3/_4$" X 5"
L (18-20)	10 $^1/_4$" X 5"	14 $^1/_2$" X 5"	15 $^1/_2$" X 5"
XL (22-24)	10 $^3/_4$" X 5"	15 $^1/_4$" X 5"	16 $^1/_4$" X 5"
XXL (26-28)	11 $^1/_8$" X 5"	16 $^1/_4$" X 5"	17 $^1/_4$" X 5"

For a more accurate fit use your arm measurements as follows:
- Measure above the elbow for the short sleeve and add 2" for the seams and ease (example: if your arm measures 11" above the elbow then the cuff will be cut 13" X 5").
- Measure below the elbow for the $^3/_4$ sleeve and add 2" for the seams and ease (example: if your arm measures 10" below the elbow then the cuff will be cut 12" X 5").
- The long sleeve cuff may be adjusted by adjusting the placement of the button.
- The instructions in Cuffs A - I are to be used on the short or $^3/_4$ sleeve.
- The instructions in J and K are to be used on the long sleeve only.

A. Cuff (For the Short or $^3/_4$ Sleeve)

1. Run two gathering rows $^1/_8$" and $^1/_4$" between the marks on each sleeve. Gather the lower edge of each sleeve between the marks to fit the cuffs. Place the cuff to the sleeve, right sides together, and stitch using a $^1/_4$" seam (fig. 24).
2. Place the blouse right sides together matching the underarm seams, cuff seams, bottom edges and stitch the side seams and sleeve seams including the cuff (fig. 25).
3. Turn the bottom edge of the cuff to the inside $^1/_4$". Fold the cuff in half and hand stitch the folded edge to the stitching line of the cuff (fig. 26).

B. Fabric Cuff with Entredeux and Gathered Edging
   (For the Short or ³/₄ Sleeve)

1. Run two gathering rows ¹/₈" and ¹/₄" between the marks on each sleeve. Gather the lower edge of the sleeve between the marks to fit the cuff. Place the cuff to the sleeves right sides together and stitch using a ¹/₄" seam (see fig. 24).
2. Turn the long edge of the cuff to the inside ¹/₄" and press. Fold the cuff in half and hand stitch the folded edge to the stitching line of the cuff (fig. 27).
3. Cut two entredeux pieces to fit the cuff measurement.
4. Cut away one side of the fabric from the entredeux.
5. Cut two pieces of edging lace twice the length of the entredeux.
6. Gather the lace to fit the entredeux. Zigzag together using the technique "gathered lace to entredeux" (fig. 28).
7. Trim away the fabric from the other side of the entredeux and attach the strip of entredeux/lace to the folded edge of the cuff by butting the entredeux to the folded edge and stitching with a zigzag stitch (fig. 29).
8. Place the sleeves and sides of the blouse right sides together and stitch a ¹/₄" seam from the lower edge of the blouse up the side and down the sleeve to the edge of the lace trim. This will be one continuous seam (fig. 30).

C. Fabric Cuff with Entredeux and Flat Edging—
   (For the Short or ³/₄ Sleeve)

Follow steps 1-4 above in B. Fabric Cuff with Extredeux and Gathered Edging.

5. Cut two pieces of edging the same length of the entredeux.
6. Attach the edging to the entredeux using the technique "lace to entredeux".
7. Follow step 7 and 8 above.

D. Fabric Cuff with Piping ———
   (For the Short or ³/₄ Sleeve)

1. Place the sides of the blouse together and stitch the side seams and sleeve seams using a ¹/₄" seam (fig. 31).
2. Cut 2 pieces of piping, one for each cuff, the same measurement as the long side of the cuff. You may use purchased piping or refer to the section on Piping and make your own piping.
3. Trim the seam allowance of the piping to ¹/₄" if it is larger than ¹/₄".
4. Place the piping along one long side of each cuff, having the raw edges even and stitch with a ¹/₄" seam slightly away from the cord of the piping (fig. 32).
5. Place the short ends of one cuff piece together matching the piping and stitch using a ¹/₄" seam. This forms a circle. Repeat for the other cuff (fig. 33).
6. Run two gathering rows ¹/₈" and ¹/₄" between the marks on each sleeve. Gather the lower edge of the sleeve between the marks to fit the circular cuff. Place the cuff to the sleeve, right sides together, with the piping sandwiched between the sleeve and the cuff. Stitch the layers together using the stitching line from step 4 as a guideline for

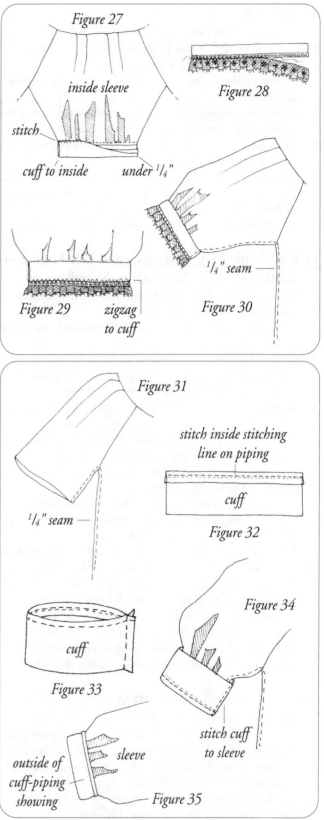

Figure 27

inside sleeve

stitch

cuff to inside   under ¹/₄"

Figure 28

Figure 29   zigzag   Figure 30
            to cuff

¹/₄" seam

Figure 31

stitch inside stitching
line on piping

cuff

Figure 32

¹/₄" seam

cuff

Figure 33

Figure 34

stitch cuff
to sleeve

outside of
cuff-piping
showing   sleeve

Figure 35

stitching. Stitch closer to the piping than you did in step 4 (fig. 34).

7. Turn the edge of the cuff to the inside ¹/₄". Fold the cuff in half (see fig. 26) and hand stitch the folded edge to the stitching line of the cuff (fig. 35).

E. Cuff With Bias
(For the Short or ³/₄ Sleeve)

1. Cut a bias strip 2" wide by the cuff measurement.
2. Fold the strip in half and press.
3. Run two gathering rows ¹/₈" and ¹/₄" between the marks on each sleeve.
4. Gather the bottom of the sleeve to fit the strip. Stitch the strip in place, raw edge to raw edge, using a ¹/₄" seam.
5. Trim seam allowance to ¹/₈" (fig. 36). Stitch the side seam of the bodice/sleeve in place.
6. With the seam allowance of the binding pressed toward the binding, fold the binding to the inside of the sleeve enclosing the seam allowance. Pin in place
7. Hand stitch the binding to the inside of the sleeve (fig. 37).

F. Cuff With Bias, Entredeux and Flat Edging or Tatting (For the Short or ³/₄ Sleeve)

1. Cut a bias strip 1³/₄" wide by the cuff measurement.
2. Fold the strip in half and press.
3. Run two gathering rows ¹/₈" and ¹/₄" between the marks on each sleeve.
4. Gather the bottom of the sleeve to fit the strip. Stitch the strip in place, raw edge to raw edge, using a ¹/₄" seam. Trim seam allowance to ¹/₈" (see fig. 36). Stitch the side seam of the bodice/sleeve in place. With the seam allowance of the binding pressed toward the binding, fold the binding to the inside of the sleeve enclosing the seam allowance. Hand stitch the binding to the inside of the sleeve (see fig. 37).
5. Cut two pieces of entredeux and two pieces of edging or tatting to the cuff measurement.
6. Cut away one side of the fabric from the entredeux.
7. Attach the edging/tatting to the entredeux using the technique "lace to entredeux" (fig. 38).
8. Trim away the fabric from the other side of the entredeux and attach the strip of entredeux/lace to the folded edge of the bias by butting the entredeux to the folded edge and stitching with a zigzag stitch much like the technique "entredeux to lace". Fold back each end of the entredeux/edging piece and stitch the folded edges together by hand. Raw edges of the entredeux/edging can be stitched to the wrong side of the sleeve entredeux/edging (fig. 39).

G. Scalloped Cuff with Tatting
(For the Short or 3/4 Sleeve)

1. Fold the cuff piece in half with right sides together and place the cuff scallop template along the folded edge at the placement line. Trace the scallop onto the cuff. Cuff may be interfaced if desired (fig. 40).
2. Stitch along the traced line. Trim the seam ¹/₄" below the stitching line and clip the curves (fig. 41).
3. Turn the cuff piece and press well. Turn under ¹/₄" on one long edge of the cuff piece. This side is now the inside of the cuff (fig. 42).
4. Run two gathering rows ¹/₈" and ¹/₄" between the marks on the bottom of each sleeve. Gather the lower edge of the

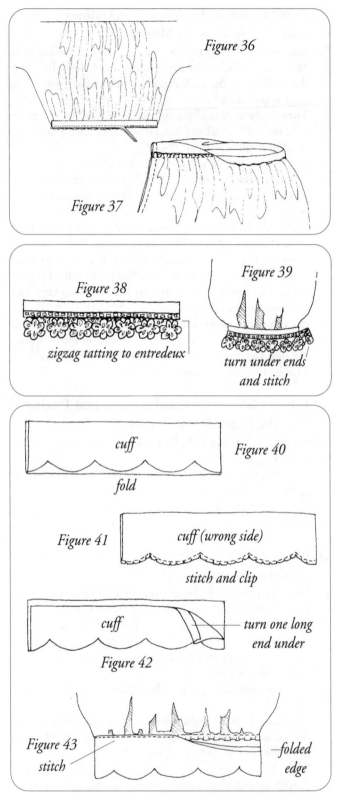

Figure 36

Figure 37

Figure 38

zigzag tatting to entredeux

Figure 39

turn under ends and stitch

cuff

Figure 40

fold

Figure 41

cuff (wrong side)

stitch and clip

cuff

turn one long end under

Figure 42

Figure 43

stitch

folded edge

sleeve between the marks to fit the cuff piece and place the gathered edge of the sleeve right sides together with the outside of the cuff. Stitch with a ¹/₄" seam. Be sure not to catch the folded edge from step 3 in the stitching. Press the seam towards the cuff.

5. Lap the ¹/₄" folded edge over the seam on the inside of the sleeve and stitch in place by hand or machine (fig. 43).

6. Butt the top edge of the tatting to the edge of the scallop of the sleeve. Hand whip in place or stitch with a zigzag (fig. 44).

7. With thread to match the blouse, stitch a medium width satin stitch along the edge of the scallop. This will cover up the stitches made when attaching the tatting (fig. 44). Water soluble stabilizer may be used under the cuff if desired.

8. Place the sleeves and sides of the blouse right sides together and stitch a $^1/_4$" seam from the lower edge of the blouse up the side and down the sleeve to the edge of the lace trim. This will be one continuous seam (fig. 45).

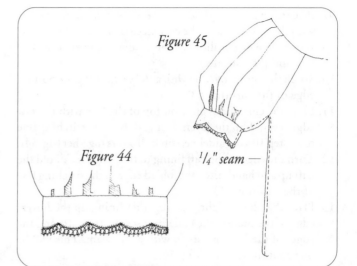

Figure 45

Figure 44

$^1/_4$" seam —

H. Fabric Cuff Covered with Lace (For the Short or $^3/_4$ Sleeve)

1. Place a piece of the wide edging onto each cuff piece, placing the top edge of the lace $^1/_4$" from the raw edge of the cuff. The wrong side of the lace will be placed to the right side of the cuff. Straight stitch in the ditch of the heading of the lace, securing the lace to the cuff (fig. 46).

2. Run two gathering rows $^1/_8$" and $^1/_4$" between the marks on the bottom of each sleeve. Gather the lower edge of each sleeve between the marks to fit the cuffs. Place the cuff to the sleeve, right sides together, and stitch using a $^1/_4$" seam. The seam stitched in step 1 may be used as a guideline for stitching the cuff to the sleeve (fig. 47).

3. Place the blouse right sides together and stitch the side seams and sleeve seams including the cuff (fig. 48).

4. Turn the edge of the cuff to the inside $^1/_4$". Fold the cuff in half and hand stitch or machine stitch the folded edge to the stitching line of the cuff (fig. 49).

I. Scalloped Bias with Pleated Lace (For the Short or $^3/_4$ Sleeve)

1. Run two gathering rows $^1/_8$" and $^1/_4$" between the marks on the bottom of each sleeve. Gather the lower edge of each sleeve between the marks to fit the cuff.

2. Fold each cuff in half and crease. Cut along the fold creating two cuff pieces for each sleeve (one cuff and one cuff lining) (fig. 50).

3. Place one cuff piece and the sleeve right sides together and stitch with a $^1/_4$" seam. The cuff may be interfaced if desired (fig. 51).

cuff

cut on fold

cuff lining

fold

Figure 50

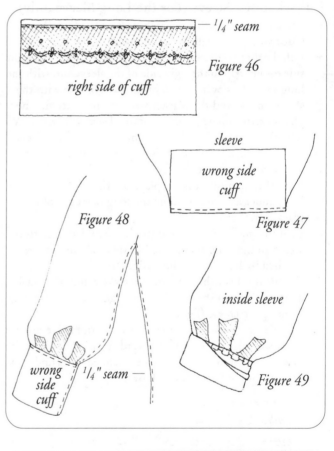

$^1/_4$" seam

Figure 46

right side of cuff

sleeve

wrong side cuff

Figure 48

Figure 47

inside sleeve

wrong side cuff

$^1/_4$" seam —

Figure 49

4. Flip the cuff down and press the seam towards the cuff.

5. Refer to the technique for making Scalloped Bias and create enough scalloped bias for the lower edge of each cuff piece.

6. Cut two pieces of scalloped bias the measurement of the long edges of the two cuff pieces.

7. Pleat a piece of lace edging the length of the cuff measurement referring to the instructions for using the Perfect Pleater.

8. Place the raw edge of the bias scallop even with the top edge of the pleated lace and stitch the two together about $^1/_8$" from the raw edge (fig. 52).

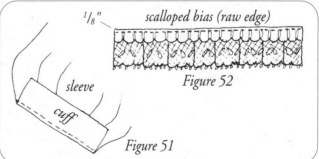

$^1/_8$"

scalloped bias (raw edge)

sleeve

Figure 52

cuff

Figure 51

9. Place the bias scallop/pleated lace piece right sides together with the lower edge of the cuff piece that is attached to the sleeve. The bias scallop will be sandwiched between the lace and the cuff piece.
10. Stitch the layers together with a ¹/₄" seam along the bottom edge of the cuff (fig. 53).
11. Place the cuff lining piece on top of the lace with the raw edges even. Flip the layers over and used the stitching line from step 10 as a guideline, stitch all layers together (fig. 54).
12. Turn the edge of the cuff lining to the inside ¹/₄". Fold the cuff up and hand stitch the folded edge to the stitching line of the cuff (fig. 55).
13. Place the blouse right sides together lining up the lower edge of the blouse, the underarm seams, the cuffs and the edges of the lace and stitch with a ¹/₄" seam. This will be one continuous seam (fig. 56).

J. Placket in a Sleeve (For the Long Sleeve only)

1. Cut a slit along the line on each sleeve 4 ¹/₄" long (fig. 57).
2. Cut two strips of fabric 1" wide by 9 ¹/₂" long.
3. Pull the slit in the sleeve apart to form a "V". Place the right side of the strip to the right side of the sleeve slit, with the long raw edges even. Stitch on the wrong side with the sleeve on top and the placket strip on the bottom. The placket strip will be straight and the sleeve will form a "V" with the point of the "V" ¹/₄" from the edge of the placket. Stitch, using a ¹/₄" seam. It is important to catch a few fibers in the seam at the point of the "V" (fig. 58).
4. Press the seam towards the placket strip.
5. Fold under a ¹/₄" seam along the long raw edge of the placket (fig. 59).
6. Fold the placket in half and stitch the folded edge from step 5 to the seam line created in step 3. This may be stitched by hand or machine (fig. 60).
7. On the inside of the placket, stitch the top of the placket at an angle from the lower inside edge to the folded edge forming a triangle (fig. 61).
8. Lay the sleeve on a flat surface with the right side up and the lower edge of the sleeve towards you. The side of the placket closest to the seam will be extended. Fold under the placket on the other side (fig. 62).

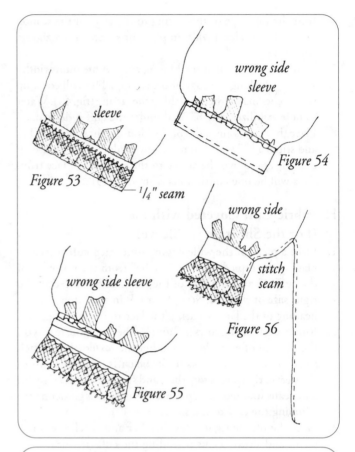

Figure 53

Figure 54

¹/₄" seam

wrong side
sleeve

sleeve

wrong side sleeve

Figure 55

wrong side

stitch
seam

Figure 56

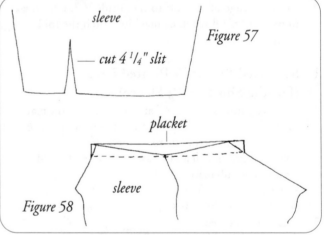

sleeve

Figure 57

cut 4 ¹/₄" slit

placket

sleeve

Figure 58

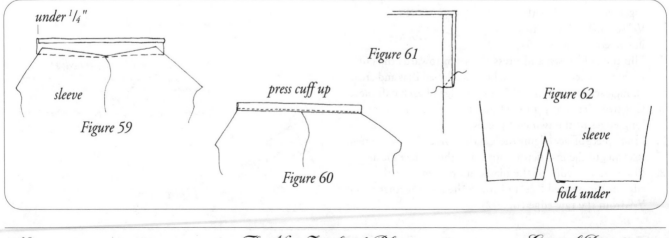

under ¹/₄"

sleeve

Figure 59

press cuff up

Figure 60

Figure 61

Figure 62

sleeve

fold under

K. Buttoned Cuff (For the Long Sleeve only)

1. Place the blouse right sides together lining up the lower edge of the blouse, the underarm seams and the sleeve. Stitch with a $^{1}/_{4}$" seam (fig. 63).
2. Run two gathering rows $^{1}/_{8}$" and $^{1}/_{4}$" in the bottom of the sleeve. Gather the sleeve to fit between the marks on the buttoned cuff (fig. 63).
3. Place the sleeve to the cuff, with right sides together pin the cuff to the sleeve edge matching the gathers to the marking on the cuff and the finished sleeve to the $^{1}/_{4}$" seam line on the cuff. Remember that the side closest to the seam will be extended and the other side folded back. Stitch with a $^{1}/_{4}$" seam. The cuff may be interfaced if desired (fig. 64).
4. Fold under $^{1}/_{4}$" along the lower long edge of the buttoned cuff and press well.
5. Fold the cuff up, right sides together, the $^{1}/_{4}$" folded edge from step 4 will fall on the seam line, and stitch a $^{1}/_{4}$" seam at each end of the cuffs (fig. 65).
6. Turn the cuff right side out, bring the folded edge from step 3 up to the seam line. Pin in place (fig. 66).
7. Press the sleeve well and top stitch the ends of the cuff and the top edge securing it near the seam line (fig. 66).
8. Center a buttonhole mark $^{1}/_{2}$" from the front edge of the cuff. Work a machine buttonhole at the mark and sew a button in the middle of the cuff just below the placket. Fit the blouse cuff, if desired, to find the button placement (fig. 66).

IV. Sleeves to Armholes

1. Trace the markings for the pleats onto the tops of the sleeves.
2. Fold the pleats into place along the lines given and pin (fig. 67). Pleats may need adjusting when attached to the yoke.
3. Place the front of the blouse and the sleeves right sides together at the armhole curve. Stitch with a $^{1}/_{4}$" seam (fig. 68).
4. Place the backs of the blouse and the sleeves right sides together at the armhole curve. Stitch with a $^{1}/_{4}$" seam (fig. 68).

V. Yoke to Blouse

A. Yoke with Entredeux

1. Measure around the outer edge of the yoke. Cut a piece of entredeux to this measurement plus 1".
2. If the fabric edge on the entredeux does not measure $^{1}/_{4}$", trim it to $^{1}/_{4}$".
3. Clip both sides of the entredeux so that it will curve.
4. The facing on the yoke and the blouse will be open.
5. Refer to the technique "entredeux to flat fabric" and attach the entredeux to the lower edge of the yoke (fig. 69).
6. Refer to the technique "entredeux to flat fabric" and attach the blouse bodice to the remaining edge of the entredeux (fig. 70).
7. Fold the facings along the back of the blouse to the wrong side along the fold lines (fig. 70).

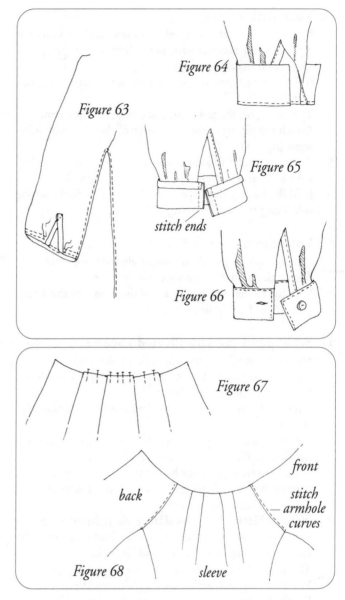

Figure 63

Figure 64

Figure 65

stitch ends

Figure 66

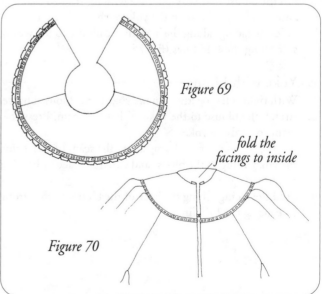

Figure 67

back

front

stitch armhole curves

Figure 68

sleeve

Figure 69

fold the facings to inside

Figure 70

B. Yoke with Piping

1. Measure around the outer edge of the yoke. Cut a piece of piping to this measurement plus 1"(refer to technique "piping" if making piping).
2. If the fabric edge on the piping does not measure $^1/_4$", trim it to $^1/_4$".
3. The facing on the yoke and the blouse will be open.
4. Attach the piping to the lower edge of the yoke with a $^1/_4$" seam (fig. 71).
5. With right sides together, attach the blouse to the yoke with a $^1/_4$" seam. Press the seam toward the yoke.
6. Fold the facings along the back of the blouse to the wrong side along the fold lines (fig. 72).

C. Yoke Seam

1. Pin the yoke to the blouse with right sides together.
2. Attach the blouse to the yoke with a $^1/_4$" seam.
3. Fold the facings along the back of the blouse to the wrong side along the fold lines (fig. 73).

D. Scalloped Bias with Pleated Lace

1. Measure around the outer edge of the yoke. Make scalloped bias strip to this measurement plus 1"(refer to II. Neck Finishes, D. Scalloped Bias).
2. If the fabric edge on the scalloped bias does not measure $^1/_4$", trim it to $^1/_4$".
3. Pleat the lace edging referring to the instructions for using the Perfect Pleater to the above measurement.
4. Place the raw edge of the bias scallop even with the top edge of the pleated lace and stitch the two together about $^1/_8$" from the raw edge (see fig. 52).
5. Place the bias scallop/pleated lace piece right sides together with the lower edge of the yoke. The bias scallop will be sandwiched between the lace and the yoke.
6. The facing on the yoke and the blouse will be open.
7. Stitch the layers together with a $^1/_4$" seam (fig. 74).
8. Pin the blouse bodice to the yoke with right sided together and attach the blouse to the yoke with a $^1/_4$" seam.
9. Fold the facings along the back of the blouse to the wrong side along the fold lines (fig. 75).

E. Yoke with Lining

1. With right sides together pin the yoke to the blouse bodice.
2. Attach the blouse to the yoke with a $^1/_4$" seam. Press the seam toward the yoke.
3. Pin the $^1/_4$" hem of the lining along the seam line securing the yoke lining to the blouse and stitch in place by hand or machine (fig. 76).
4. Fold the facings along the back of the blouse to the wrong side along the fold lines.

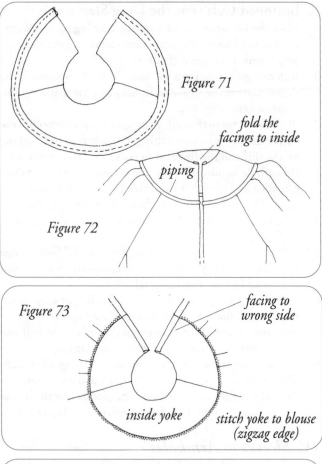

Figure 71

fold the facings to inside

piping

Figure 72

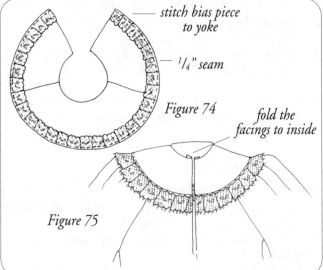

Figure 73

facing to wrong side

inside yoke

stitch yoke to blouse (zigzag edge)

stitch bias piece to yoke

$^1/_4$" seam

Figure 74

fold the facings to inside

Figure 75

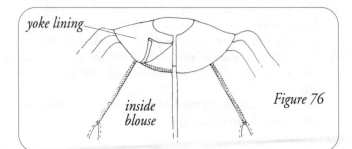

yoke lining

inside blouse

Figure 76

VI. Hemming the Blouse

1. With the facings open, fold up ¹/₄" and press. Fold up ¹/₄" again and press, creating a narrow hem. Fold facings along the fold line and stitch the hem in place (fig. 77).

VII. Finishing the Back with Buttonholes

1. Position a buttonhole at the top and bottom of the yoke on the left hand side by placing a dot ¹/₂" from the top fabric edge of the neckline and ¹/₂" over from the fold line of the yoke. Place a dot ⁵/₈" up from the yoke seam and ¹/₂" over from the fold line.
2. Place a dot every 4" down the back of the blouse ¹/₂" from the fold (fig. 78).
3. Stitch a ¹/₂" buttonhole beginning the top of the buttonhole at the dot and placing the buttonholes vertically. Continue the buttonholes down the back of the blouse. Cut the buttonholes open with a buttonhole cutter or seam ripper.
4. Lap the left side of the blouse over the right side and mark the placement for the buttons (fig. 78).
5. Attach buttons along the marks on the right side of the blouse (fig. 78).

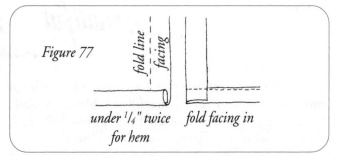

Figure 77

fold line   facing

under ¹/₄" twice   fold facing in
for hem

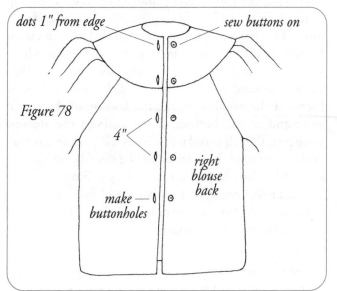

dots 1" from edge   sew buttons on

Figure 78

4"

make — buttonholes

right blouse back

Beautiful Beaded Bows

Pink silk dupioni with ecru laces and silk ribbon embroidery are used for this magnificent blouse. Slightly off center is the ecru French beading bow which is threaded with a burgundy silk ribbon on the round yoke. Gorgeous silk ribbon embroidery is done on top of this bow in shades of blue, lavender, cream and pale pink. The stems are featherstitch and there are cream French knots scattered throughout the embroidery. Beading threaded with the burgundy ribbon is flip-flopped around to the center back. Ecru entredeux is found at the neckline, along the bottom of the round yoke and at the bottom of the cuff on the sleeves. Gathered French ecru lace finishes the neckline as well as the bottom of the each cuff. The same beautiful lace shaped beading bow and embroidery is found on each sleeve. I believe this blouse is worthy of inclusion in the costume collection of any museum! The back is closed with buttons and buttonholes.

Beautiful Beaded Bows

Directions

Follow the General Blouse Directions found on page 5. Embellishment directions are given below.

Materials Needed

- 3$^1/_4$ yards - 45" wide fabric
- 3$^1/_2$ yards of entredeux
- 5$^1/_3$ yards of ecru lace beading
- $^1/_8$ yard of interfacing (optional)
- 6 buttons
- Silk ribbon in the following colors; 4mm; lt. pink, cream, and 5$^1/_3$ yards of pink several shades darker than the fabric, 7mm; blue, lavender
- Floss in the following colors; green, metallic
- Wash-out marker

The following pattern pieces are needed for this blouse and are found on the pull-out section: Yoke front, yoke back, blouse front, blouse back and sleeve. Refer to the General Directions, III. Finishing the Sleeve, Cuff Chart for the measurement of the $^3/_4$ Length Sleeve.

The following templates are needed for this blouse and are found on the pull-out section: Yoke silk ribbon embroidery template and sleeve silk ribbon embroidery template.

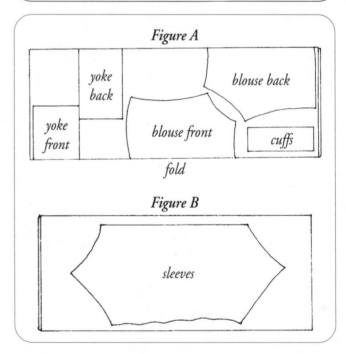

Figure A

yoke back

yoke front

blouse back

blouse front

cuffs

fold

Figure B

sleeves

Layout and Cutting

Cut out the following (Figure A & B):
- One blouse front on the fold,
- two blouse backs on the selvage
- two $^3/_4$ length sleeves
- two cuffs
- rectangle large enough on which to draw the yoke front
- rectangle large enough for each of the yoke backs

Embellishing the Yoke

1. Trace one front yoke and two back yokes onto the rectangles of fabric.
2. Cut out along the shoulder line only.
3. Place the front yoke and the back yokes right sides together and stitch the shoulder seams with a ¼" seam. Mark the center front of the yoke(fig. 1).
4. Center the yoke on the lace shaping template and trace the design on the yoke.
5. Run the silk ribbon through the lace beading. Shape the lace beading on the traced design, referring to the technique "lace shaping" (fig. 2). Stitch with a narrow zigzag.
6. Trace the silk ribbon embroidery design on the bow centering the design (fig. 3).
7. Refer to the section on silk ribbon embroidery and the embroidery template and embroider the flowers onto the yoke.
8. Cut out the yoke.

Neck Finish

Refer to the General Blouse Directions, II. Neck Finishes, A. Entredeux to Gathered Edging Lace and complete the neckline of the yoke.

Sleeves and Cuffs

1. Mark the center of each sleeve and trace the lace shaping template on each sleeve
2. With the remainder of the beading with silk ribbon, shape the beading on the traced design referring to the technique "lace shaping". Stitch with a narrow zigzag.
3. Trace the silk ribbon embroidery template in the center of the lace bow on each sleeve.
4. Refer to the section on silk ribbon embroidery and complete the embroidery according to the template.
5. Refer to the General Blouse Directions, IV. Sleeves to Armholes and attach the sleeves to the armhole.
6. Refer to the General Blouse Directions, III. Finishing the Sleeve, B. Fabric Cuff with Entredeux and Gathered Edging and complete the cuffs and attach them to the sleeves.

Completing the Blouse

1. Refer to the General Blouse Directions, V. Yoke to Blouse, A. Yoke with Entredeux and attach the yoke to the blouse.
2. Refer to the General Blouse Directions, VII. Hemming the Blouse, and finish the lower edge of the blouse.
3. Refer to the General Blouse Directions, VI. Finishing the Back with Buttonholes and complete the back of the blouse.

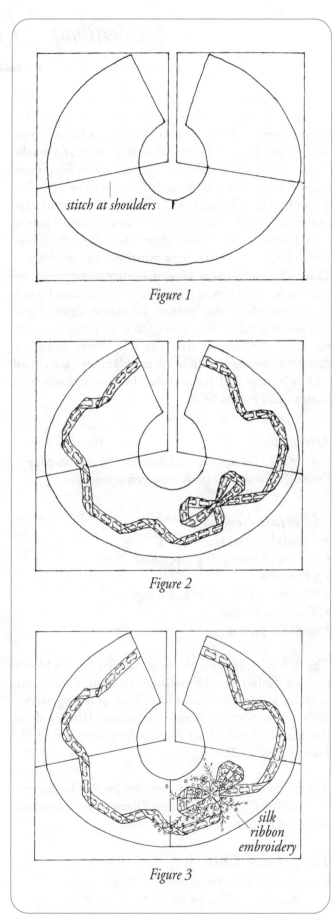

stitch at shoulders

Figure 1

Figure 2

silk ribbon embroidery

Figure 3

Cascading Lace Diamonds

Around 1920 ladies began to go on automobile outings and they wore heavy white linen clothing. This blouse seems to be the perfect automobile blouse to go along with a beautiful heavy white linen skirt and maybe a "car coat." I think the term "car coat" came from these original coats which were made to be worn in a Model-T automobile. The neckline, as well as the bottom edge of the round yoke, has heavy self fabric piping. There is a small ecru French lace diamond shaped on the center front of the yoke; it has been pinstitched to the blouse. Three $^3/_8$" tucks have been delicately pinstitched on either side of the blouse front. The beautiful ecru French lace diamonds on the front of the blouse feature three diamonds stitched like Celtic lace shaping; they are gorgeous. The sleeves have the same three cascading diamonds on them. The cuffs are plain and are closed with a button and buttonhole. The back closes with buttons and buttonholes.

Directions

Follow the General Blouse Directions found on page 5. Embellishment directions are given below.

Materials Needed

- 4 yards - 45" wide
- $^1/_8$ yard of interfacing (optional)
- 6 buttons
- $7^1/_2$ yards of $^5/_8$" wide lace insertion
- Wash-out marker
- Cord for piping

The following pattern pieces are needed for this blouse and are found on the pull-out section: Yoke front, yoke back, blouse front, blouse back and long sleeve. Refer to the General Blouse Directions, III. Finishing the Sleeve, Cuff Chart for the measurement of the Long Sleeve Cuff.

The following templates are needed for this blouse and are found on the pull-out section: Diamond yoke template, diamond bodice and sleeve template.

Layout and Cutting

Cut out the following (Figures A & B):
- two yoke fronts on the fold

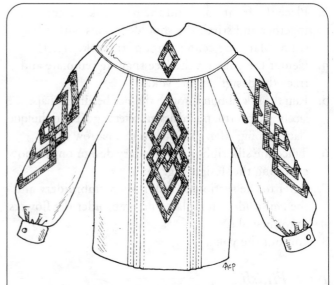

Cascading Lace Diamonds

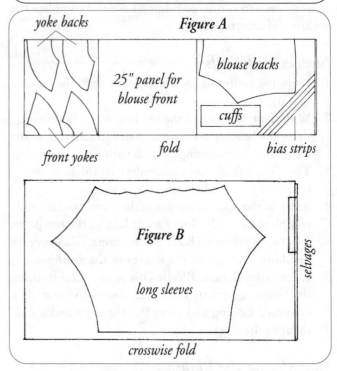

- four yoke backs on the selvage
- two blouse backs on the selvage
- two long sleeves
- two cuffs
- panel of fabric 25" down the selvage by the width of the fabric for the blouse front
- 90" of 1" bias strips to cover piping
- 2 strips 1" by $9^1/_2$" for plackets in sleeves

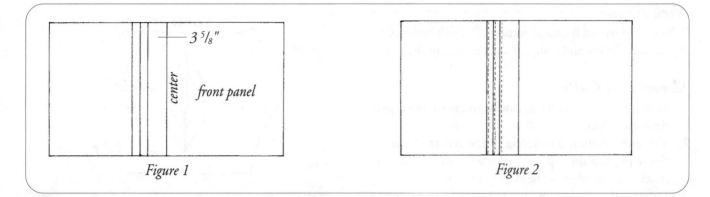

Figure 1

Figure 2

Creating the blouse front

1. On the panel of fabric for the front, mark the center front the entire length of the panel (fig. 1).
2. Measure over $3\,^5/_8$" to the left of the center and draw a line down the panel (fig. 1).
3. From the line drawn in step 2, measure over $1\,^1/_2$" and draw a line down the panel (fig. 1).
4. From the line drawn in step 3, measure over $1\,^1/_2$" and draw a line down the panel (fig. 1).
5. Fold and press along each of the three lines drawn.
6. To make the tucks, straight stitch $^3/_8$" from the fold through both thickness down the length of the panel (fig. 2).
7. Press the tucks away from the center.
8. Repeat steps 2 - 7 to the right of the center.
9. Add a decorative pin stitch done in ecru thread on each pintuck (fig. 3).
10. Fold the panel down the center line and cut one blouse front from the panel (fig. 4).
11. Trace the blouse front template between the tucks, placing the top point of the top diamond $^7/_8$" from the top edge of the blouse front (fig. 5).
12. Refer to the section on Shaping Lace Diamonds and shape the diamond design on the blouse front. Stitch the diamonds to the fabric with a small zigzag or pinstitch in ecru thread. (Cut the fabric from behind the lace.)

Embellishing the Yoke

1. Mark the center of the yoke and center the diamond template for the yoke in the center of the yoke (fig. 6).
2. Refer to the section on Shaping Lace Diamonds and shape the diamond design on the yoke. Stitch the diamonds with a small zigzag or pin stitch in ecru thread. (Cut the fabric from behind the lace.)
3. Refer to the section on Making Piping and make enough piping to fit around the neck and lower yoke.

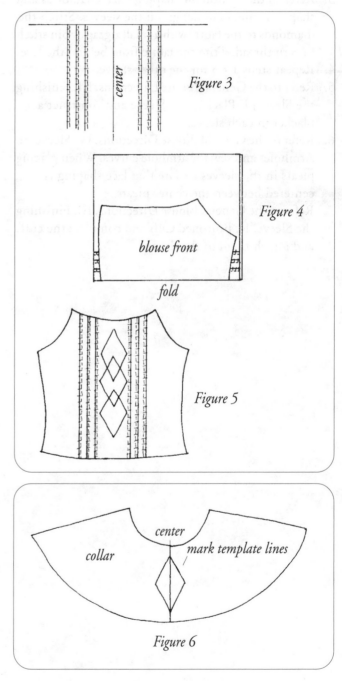

Figure 3

Figure 4

Figure 5

Figure 6

Neck Finish

Refer to the General Blouse Directions, II. Neck Finishes, C. Piping with Facing and complete the neckline of the yoke.

Sleeves and Cuffs

1. Fold the sleeve in half lengthwise and mark the center down the fold.
2. Trace the diamond template in the center of the sleeve placing the top point of the top diamond $3^5/_8$" from the top edge of the sleeve (fig. 7).
3. Refer to the section on Shaping Lace Diamonds and shape the diamond design on the sleeves. Stitch the diamonds to the fabric with a small zigzag or pin stitch in ecru thread. Trim the fabric from behind the lace.
4. Repeat steps 1 - 3 for the other sleeve.
5. Refer to the General Blouse Directions, III. Finishing the Sleeve, J. Placket in a Sleeve and construct a placket in each sleeve.
6. Refer to the General Blouse Directions, IV. Sleeves to Armholes and sew the armhole curves. When placing pleats in the sleeves be sure that lace shaping is centered between the center pleats.
7. Refer to the General Blouse Directions, III. Finishing the Sleeve, K. Buttoned Cuff and complete the cuffs and attach them to the sleeve.

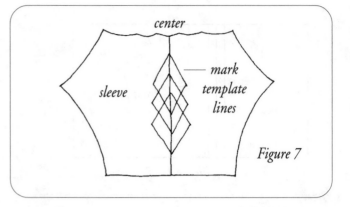

Figure 7

Completing the Blouse

1. Refer to the General Blouse Directions, V. Yoke to Blouse, B. Yoke with Piping, and attach the yoke to the blouse.
2. Refer to the General Blouse Directions, V. Yoke to Blouse, E. Yoke with Lining steps 3 and 4 and secure lining to yoke seam.
3. Refer to the General Blouse Directions, VI. Hemming the Blouse, and finish the lower edge of the blouse.
4. Refer to the General Blouse Directions, VII. Finishing the Back with Buttonholes and complete the back of the blouse.

Creative Cutwork with Tatting

"Tailored Elegance" is the perfect description for this beautiful blouse of pink linen with delicate triple looped tatting. Smooth flowing lines of cutwork on the collar front curve nicely around the scalloped edge. The tatted edging seems to "peek-out" from behind the smooth satin stitching which edges the collar. Crisp folded pleats on the sleeves gather into cuffs, which are also edged with satin stitching and tatting. This blouse can be used as a transitional piece when paired with a printed skirt for a casual daytime look or with a solid long skirt for a dressier evening ensemble. Buttons and buttonholes close the back of the blouse.

Creative Cutwork with Tatting

Directions

Follow the General Blouse Directions found on page 5. Embellishment directions are given below.

Materials Needed

- 4 yards - 45" wide fabric
- $^1/_8$ yard of interfacing (optional)
- 6 buttons
- 3 yards of $^1/_2$" wide tatted edging
- Water Soluble Stabilizer (WSS)
- Decorative rayon thread for cutwork and satin stitching
- Wash-out marker

The following pattern pieces are needed for this blouse and are found on the pull-out section: Yoke front, yoke back, collar front, collar back, blouse front, blouse back and $^3/_4$ length sleeve. Refer to the General Blouse Directions, III. Finishing the Sleeve, Cuff Chart for the measurement of the $^3/_4$ Length Cuff.

The following templates are needed for this blouse and are found on the pull-out section: Scallop template for collar, scallop template for cuffs and cutwork template for collar.

Layout and Cutting

Cut out the following (Figures A & B):
- One yoke front on the fold
- two yoke backs on the selvage
- one blouse front on the fold
- two blouse backs on the selvage

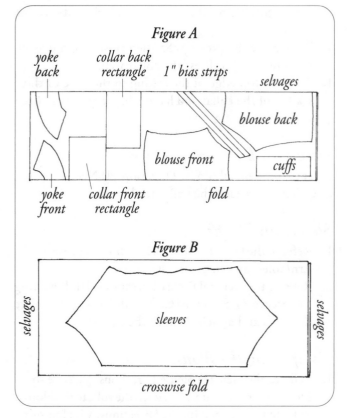

Figure A

yoke back   collar back rectangle   1" bias strips   selvages

blouse back

blouse front

cuffs

yoke front   collar front rectangle   fold

Figure B

selvages   sleeves   selvages

crosswise fold

- two $^3/_4$ length sleeves
- two cuffs
- rectangle large enough on which to draw the collar front
- two rectangles large enough for each of the collar backs
- bias strip 1" by 23" to be used to attach the collar

Embellishing the Collar

1. Trace the blouse collar front onto the rectangle of fabric just larger than the pattern piece and trace two blouse collar backs onto the rectangles of fabric (fig. 1).
2. Cut out the collars along the shoulder seams only and sew the front collar to the back collars.
3. Trace the scallop template onto the collar placing the inside points of the scallop along the outer curve of the collar (fig. 2).
4. Trace the cutwork template onto the blouse collar (fig. 2).
5. Refer to the section on Cutwork and complete the cutwork design (fig. 3).
6. Iron several layers of WSS together to use as a stabilizer behind the scallop edge of the collar. Strips of WSS may be used, as long as the strips fit behind the design.
7. Place a WSS strip at the back neck edge of the collar behind the drawn scalloped line.
8. Zigzag along the scalloped line with a small zigzag.
9. Trim away only the fabric very close to the zigzag. Do not trim the WSS (fig. 4).
10. Stitch a wide satin stitch over the zigzag so that the needle stitches off the edge of the fabric and into the WSS.
11. Trim away the excess WSS then rinse to remove all remaining WSS. Press the collar well.
12. Butt the top edge of the tatting to the edge of the scallop of the collar and hand whip in place or stitch with a zigzag (fig. 5).

Neck Finish

Refer to the General Blouse Directions, II Neck Finishes, E. Collar and attach the collar to the yoke.

Sleeves and Cuffs

1. Refer to the General Blouse Directions, IV. Sleeves to Armholes, and insert the sleeves.
2. Refer to the General Blouse Directions, III. Finishing The Sleeve, G. Scalloped Cuff With Tatting, complete the cuffs and attach them to the sleeves.

Completing the Blouse

1. Refer to the General Blouse Directions, V. Yoke to Blouse, C. Yoke Seam, and attach the yoke to the blouse.
2. Refer to the General Blouse Directions, VI. Hemming the Blouse, and finish the lower edge of the blouse.
3. Refer to the General Blouse Directions, VII. Finishing the Back with Buttonholes and complete the back of the blouse.

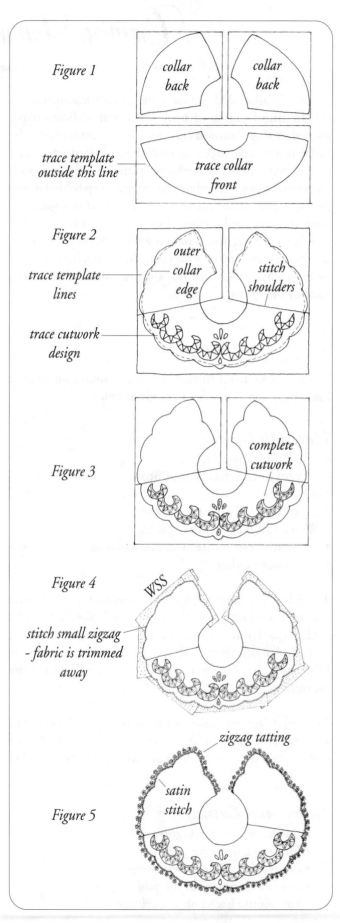

Figure 1

collar back

collar back

trace template outside this line

trace collar front

Figure 2

trace template lines

outer collar edge

stitch shoulders

trace cutwork design

Figure 3

complete cutwork

Figure 4

WSS

stitch small zigzag - fabric is trimmed away

Figure 5

zigzag tatting

satin stitch

Lace Diamond Delight

What could be more beautiful than ice blue silk dupioni with ecru lace diamonds and silk ribbon embroidery in shades of green, pink, lavender, dusty lavender and green? This wonderful blouse has small ecru antique lace diamonds meeting end to end traveling all the way around the yoke. The silk ribbon flower bouquets have six petals; two pink, two white and two lavender. The stems are green with green leaves at the bottom of each stem. Several yellow French knots and purple straight stitches finish the inside of each flower. Such wonderful silk ribbon embroidery! The diamonds are pinstitched to the yoke and there is beautiful piping used around the top and the bottom of the yoke. Three pleats gather in the fullness of the sleeves. Buttons and buttonholes close the back.

Directions

Follow the General Blouse Directions found on page 5. Embellishment directions are given below.

Materials Needed

- $3^2/_3$ yards - 45" wide fabric
- $^1/_8$ yard of interfacing (optional)
- 6 buttons
- 3 yards of cord for making piping
- 3 yards of $^5/_8$" wide lace insertion
- Wing needle for pin stitching (optional)
- Silk ribbon in the following colors: 4mm- two shades of pink, one of lavender; 7mm- two shades of pink, one of lavender, one of green
- Floss in the following colors: green, gold, and black Wash-out marker

The following pattern pieces are needed for this blouse and are found on the pull-out section: Yoke front, yoke back, blouse front, blouse back and short sleeve. Refer to the General Blouse Directions, III. Finishing the sleeve, cuff chart for the measurement of the short sleeve cuff.

The following template is needed for this blouse and is found on the pull-out section: Diamond template for yoke with silk ribbon embroidery.

Layout and Cutting

Cut out the following (Figures A and B):
- One yoke front on the fold for lining

Lace Diamond Delight

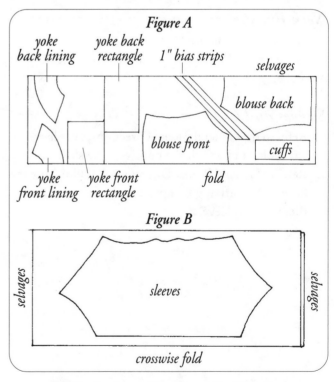

- two yoke backs on the selvage for lining
- one blouse front on the fold
- two blouse backs on the selvage
- two short sleeves, two cuffs
- rectangle large enough on which to draw the yoke front
- two rectangles large enough for each of the yoke backs
- $2^1/_2$ yards of 1" bias for piping

Embellishing the Yoke

1. Trace one front yoke and two back yokes on the rectangles of fabric.
2. Cut out along the shoulder line only.
3. Place the front yoke and the back yokes right sides together and stitch the shoulder seams. Mark the center front of the yoke.
4. Trace the diamond template design and the silk ribbon embroidery design onto the yoke centering one diamond at the center of the yoke (fig. 1).
5. Refer to lace shaping techniques and shape the lace into the diamond shapes. Zigzag or pinstitch around the lace shapes (fig. 2).
6. Refer to the section on silk ribbon embroidery and the embroidery template and embroider the flowers onto the lower portion of the yoke (fig. 2).
7. Cut out the yoke.
8. Refer to the technique "Piping" and make enough piping to fit around the neck and lower yoke approximately $2^{1}/_{2}$ yards.

Neck Finish

Refer to General Blouse Directions, II. Neck Finishes, C. Piping with Facing and complete the neckline of the yoke.

Sleeves and Cuffs

1. Refer to the General Blouse Directions, IV. Sleeves to Armholes and attach the bodice to the sleeves.
2. Refer to General Blouse Directions, III. Finishing the Sleeve, A. Cuff and complete the cuffs and attach them to the sleeves.

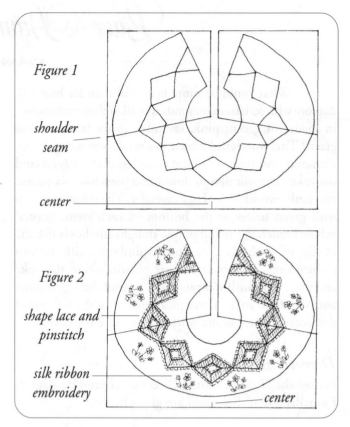

Figure 1

shoulder seam

center

Figure 2

shape lace and pinstitch

silk ribbon embroidery

center

Completing the Blouse

1. Refer to General Blouse Directions, V. Yoke to Blouse, B. Yoke with Piping, and attach the yoke to the blouse. Refer to the General Blouse Directions, E. Yoke with Lining, steps 3 and 4, and attach lining to yoke seam.
2. Refer to General Blouse Directions, VI. Hemming the Blouse, and finish the lower edge of the blouse.
3. Refer to General Blouse Directions, VII. Finishing the Back with Buttonholes and complete the back of the blouse.

Seafoam Lace Blouse

Call it seafoam or robin's egg blue, either is correct. For those who love tailored heirloom, this blouse fits the bill with its pleated French lace. This Swiss batiste seafoam fabric has a delicate windowpane design. The blouse features a very unusual pleated white French lace around the round yoke as well as the bottom of the sleeve cuff. Scalloped piping of the same fabric as the blouse is used around the neckline, the bottom of the yoke and the cuffs. The back is closed with buttons and buttonholes.

Directions

Follow the General Blouse Directions found on page 5. Embellishment directions are given below.

Materials Needed

- $3^2/_3$ yards of 45" wide fabric
- $7^1/_4$ yards of 2" lace edging
- Perfect Pleater
- $1/_8$ yard of interfacing for cuff (optional)
- 6 Buttons
- Thread to match the fabric

The following pattern pieces are needed for this blouse and are found on the pull-out section: Yoke front, yoke back, blouse front, blouse back and $3/_4$ length sleeve. Refer to the General Blouse Directions, III. Finishing the Sleeve, Cuff Chart for the measurement of the $3/_4$ Length Cuff.

The technique for making the Scalloped Bias is found in General Blouse Directions, II Neck Finishes, D. Scalloped Bias. The directions for the Perfect Pleater are included with the Perfect Pleater.

Layout and Cutting

The fabric used for the blouse that is pictured had a squared color on color pattern design. The yoke of the blouse was cut on the bias both back and front. If using a fabric with a design that will show up on the bias, we suggest that you cut the yoke on the bias.

Cut out the following (Figures A & B):
- One yoke front on the fold for the lining
- two back yokes on the selvage for the lining
- one yoke front on the bias folded
- two yoke backs on the bias (if using a plain fabric

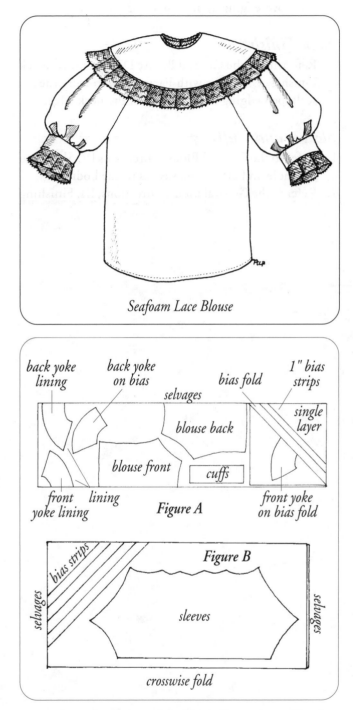

Seafoam Lace Blouse

Figure A

Figure B

where the design of the bias will not show, all yokes may be cut on the straight of the grain)
- one blouse front on the fold
- two blouse backs on the selvage
- two $3/_4$ sleeves
- two cuffs
- 3 yards of $1^1/_2$" bias for scalloped edging.

Embellishing the blouse

1. Referring to the General Blouse Directions, II. Neck Finishes, D. Scalloped Bias and prepare a piece of scalloped edging approximately 3 yards long.

Neck Finish

1. Referring to the General Blouse Directions, II. Neck Finishes, C. Piping with Facing and treating the scalloped edging as piping finish the neck edge.

Sleeves and Cuffs

1. Refer to the General Blouse Directions IV. Sleeves to Armhole and attach the sleeves to the bodice.
2. Refer to the General Blouse Directions, III. Finishing the Sleeves, I. Scalloped Bias with Pleated Lace and attach and embellish the cuff.

Completing the Blouse

1. Referring to the General Blouse Directions, V. Yoke to Blouse, D. Scalloped Bias with Pleated Lace embellish the yoke and attach the bodice.
2. Referring to the General Blouse Directions, V. Yoke to Blouse, E. Yoke with Lining steps 3 and 4 and attach the yoke lining to the blouse.
3. Referring to the General Blouse Directions, VI. Hemming the Blouse, hem the bottom of the blouse.
4. Referring to the General Blouse Directions, VII. Finishing the Back with Buttonholes, finish the back of the blouse.

Silk Ribbon Bows and Flowers

"Dreams of loveliness" are found in this masterpiece of silk ribbon embroidery on pink linen. The roses are stitched in three shades of pink. The forget-me-knots around the clusters of flowers are pale blue. Green stems and leaves finish the flower bouquets. Beautiful dark pink silk ribbon bows have been shaped on each shoulder and they are stitched down with pink silk ribbon French knots. Beautiful silk ribbon embroidery extends around the center back of the blouse. The round yoke is lined. There is a tailored cuff on the sleeves and it has been topstitched at both the top and the bottom. The back closes with buttons and buttonholes. What a masterpiece of elegance!

Silk Ribbon Bows and Flowers

Directions

Follow the General Blouse Directions found on page 5. Embellishment directions are given below.

Materials Needed

- 3 yards - 45" wide fabric
- 1/3 yard of pink batiste for lining
- 1/8 yard of interfacing (optional)
- 6 buttons
- Silk ribbon - 4mm; three shades of pink, two shades of green, one of blue
- Floss - dark pink, green
- Wash-out marker

The following pattern pieces are needed for this blouse and are found on the pull-out section: Yoke front, yoke back, blouse front, blouse back and short sleeve. Refer to the General Blouse Directions, III. Finishing the Sleeve Cuff Chart for the measurement of the short sleeve cuff.

The following template is needed for this blouse and is found on the pull-out section: Silk ribbon embroidery template

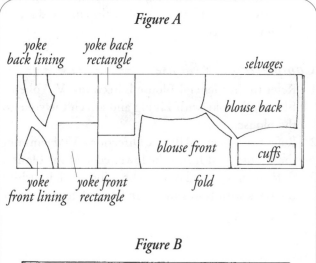

Figure A

yoke back lining · yoke back rectangle · selvages · blouse back · blouse front · cuffs · yoke front lining · yoke front rectangle · fold

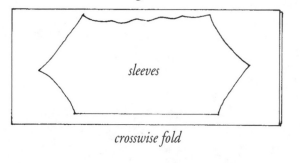

Figure B

sleeves

crosswise fold

Layout and Cutting

Cut out the following: (Figures A & B)
- One blouse front on the fold
- two blouse backs on the selvage
- two short sleeves, two cuffs
- rectangle large enough on which to draw the yoke front
- rectangle large enough for each of the yoke backs
- one front yoke on the fold
- 2 back yokes on the selvage for the lining

Embellishing the Yoke

1. Trace one front yoke and two back yokes onto the rectangles of fabric.
2. Cut out along the shoulder line only (fig. 1).
3. Place the front yoke and the back yokes right sides together and stitch the shoulder seams. Mark the center front of the yoke (fig. 2).
4. Trace the silk ribbon embroidery design onto the yoke centering the design (fig. 3).
5. Refer to the section on silk ribbon embroidery and the embroidery template and embroider the flowers onto the yoke.
6. Cut out yoke.

Neck Finish

Refer to the General Blouse Directions, II. Neck Finishes, F. Lined Yoke and complete the neckline of the yoke.

Sleeves and Cuffs

1. Refer to the General Blouse Directions, IV. Sleeves to Armholes and complete the sleeves.
2. Refer to the General Blouse Directions, III. Finishing the Sleeve, A. Cuff and complete the cuffs and attach them to the sleeves.

Completing the Blouse

1. Refer to the General Blouse Directions, V. Yoke to Blouse, E. Yoke with Lining and attach the yoke to the blouse.
2. Refer to the General Blouse Directions, VI. Hemming the Blouse, and finish the lower edge of the blouse.
3. Refer to the General Blouse Directions, VII. Finishing the Back with Buttonholes and complete the back of the blouse.

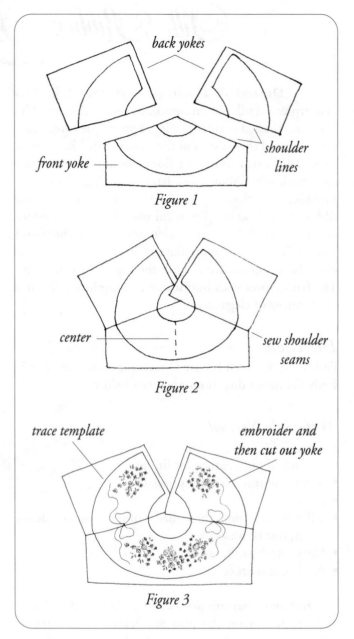

back yokes

front yoke

shoulder lines

Figure 1

center

sew shoulder seams

Figure 2

trace template

embroider and then cut out yoke

Figure 3

Silk Ribbon Embroidery and Beading Bows

I adore French beading intertwined with silk ribbon and shaped into lace shapes. In this cream colored linen blouse there is a magnificent beading lace shaped bow on the front with swirls of the lace shaped beading all the way around to the back of the blouse. The beading is white and it is pinstitched to the blouse round yoke with off-white thread. Medium pink silk ribbon is threaded through the beading. The colors of the silk ribbon embroidery are several shades of pink, blue, green and yellow. The silk ribbon is held into place in the beading by tiny French knots. The gorgeous silk ribbon embellishment is just as beautiful in the back of the blouse as it is in the front. The blouse has tailored cuffs and is closed in the back with buttons and buttonholes.

Silk Ribbon Embroidery and Beading Bows

Directions

Follow the General Blouse Directions found on page 5. Embellishment directions are given below.

Materials Needed

- $2^7/_8$ yards of 45" wide fabric
- 6 Buttons for the back of the blouse
- $2^1/_2$ yards of $^5/_8$" lace beading
- $2^1/_2$ yards of $^1/_4$" Silk Ribbon to weave through the beading
- 4mm Silk Ribbon for embroidery in the following colors: 4 shades of pink, 1 of each of the following; blue, green, peach, yellow

The following pattern pieces are needed for the blouse and are found on the pull-out section: Yoke front, yoke back, blouse front, blouse back and short sleeve. Refer to the General Blouse Directions, III. Finishing the Sleeve, cuff chart for the measurement of the short sleeve cuff.

The following template is needed for this blouse and is found on the pull-out section: Silk Ribbon Embroidery and Beading Bows template

Layout and Cutting

Cut out the following (Figure A & B):
- Two yoke front on the fold (one will be used as a lining)
- four yoke backs on the selvage (two will be used as a lining)

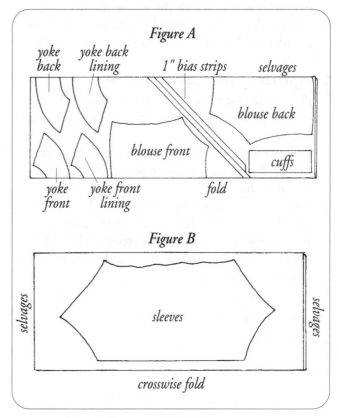

Figure A

yoke back · yoke back lining · 1" bias strips · selvages · blouse back · blouse front · cuffs · yoke front · yoke front lining · fold

Figure B

selvages · sleeves · selvages · crosswise fold

- one blouse front on the fold
- two blouse backs on the selvage
- two short sleeves
- two short sleeve cuffs
- 80" of 1" bias strips for piping

Embellishing the Yoke

1. Mark the center of the yoke front, place the right side of the yoke front to the right side of the yoke back and sew the shoulder seams with a $1/4$" seam. Center the yoke on the template and trace the design on the yoke.
2. Thread the silk ribbon through the beading. Shape the lace beading on the traced design, referring to the technique "lace shaping". Stitch the lace to the yoke using an entredeux stitch (fig. 1).
3. Secure the silk ribbon in place with French knots (fig. 2). The ribbon may be twisted under the beading to make it lay flat in the beading if necessary.
4. Embroider the silk ribbon garland around the yoke (fig. 3).

Neck Finish

1. Finish neck edge referring to the General Blouse Directions, II. Neck Finishes, C. Piping with Facing.

Sleeves and Cuffs

1. Refer to the General Blouse Directions, IV. Sleeves to Armholes and attach the bodice to the sleeve.
2. Refer to the General Blouse Directions, III. Finishing the Sleeve, A. Cuff and attach the cuff to the sleeve.

Completing the Blouse

1. Refer to the General Blouse Directions, V. Yoke to Blouse, B. Yoke with Piping and attach the bodice to the yoke.
2. Refer to the General Blouse Directions, V. Yoke to Blouse, E. Yoke with Lining step 3 and attach the lining to the yoke seam.
3. Refer to the General Blouse Directions, VI. Hemming the Blouse and hem the bottom of the blouse.
4. Refer to the General Blouse Directions, VII. Finishing the Back with Buttonholes and make buttonholes and sew on buttons.

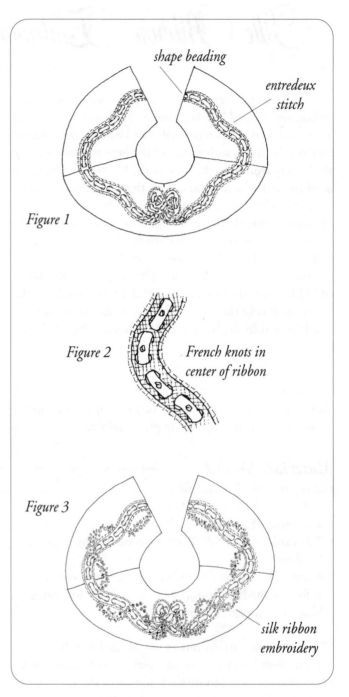

shape beading

entredeux stitch

Figure 1

Figure 2

French knots in center of ribbon

Figure 3

silk ribbon embroidery

A Touch of Smocking

Talk about elegant smocking for women! This blouse has tailored insets in the round yoke. Smocking gathers the bottom of each sleeve and is attached to a bias binding. A narrow bias binding finishes the neckline and there is piping around the bottom of the yoke and on both sides of the smocked insets. Delicate hand embroidery fills the center section; however, this would be a great place to use your wonderful embroidery machines also! The back closes with buttons and buttonholes.

Directions

Follow the General Blouse Directions found on page 5. Embellishment directions are given below.

Materials Needed

- 3$\frac{1}{3}$ yards of 45" fabric
- Cord for Piping
- Floss for smocking and embroidery
- 6 Buttons
- Fabric pleater
- Wash-out marker

The following pattern pieces are needed for this blouse and are found on the pull-out section: Front yoke, back yoke, front bodice, back bodice and $\frac{3}{4}$ sleeve. Refer to the General Blouse Directions, III. Finishing the Sleeve, Cuff Chart for the measurement of the $\frac{3}{4}$ Length Cuff.

The following templates and graphs are needed for this blouse and are found on the pull-out section or at the end of these directions: Sleeve smocking graph, monogram embroidery template, yoke smocking graph.

Layout and Cutting

Cut out the following (Figure A):
- 1 front yoke on the fold
- 2 back yokes on the selvage
- 2 blouse backs on the selvage
- one blouse front on the fold

Refold the remaining fabric and cut (Figure B):
- 2 sleeves
- 2 strips for smocking 3" x 24".
- bias to yield 2$\frac{1}{2}$ yards of 1" bias for piping
- 1$\frac{1}{2}$ yards of 2" bias for binding

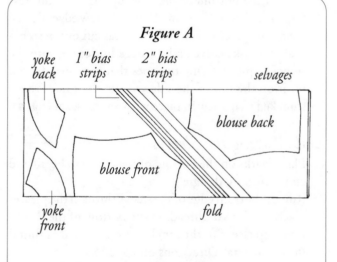

A Touch of Smocking

Figure A

yoke back   1" bias strips   2" bias strips   selvages

blouse back

blouse front

yoke front   fold

Figure B

selvages

sleeves

selvages

strips for smocking

crosswise fold

Embellishing the Yoke

1. Mark center of yoke front. Mark cutting lines for smocked yoke insertion. Center yoke over embroidery design with the top neck edge of the blouse 1" above the top of the design. Trace embroidery design onto the yoke (fig. 1).
2. Referring to the techniques on Hand Embroidery, embroider the design onto the yoke.
3. Make two strips for smocking by running 7 rows of smocking threads in each of the two 3" by 24" strips. Block the strips to 8" long. Smock the strips using the yoke smocking graph.
4. Refer to the technique on Making Piping and make a strip of piping 34" long. Trim piping seam line to $^1/_8$". Place the finished piping edge above and below the top and bottom cable rows on the smocked pieces. Sew in place. Trim smocking to the $^1/_8$" seam allowance (fig. 2).
5. Cut the yoke apart on the cutting lines. Save the piece that you cut out to refer to later (fig. 3).
6. Attach a smocked strip to each side of the yoke center front piece. Line the raw edge of the strip and the raw edge of the bottom of the yoke up together and sew together with an $^1/_8$" seam. Finish the raw edge (fig. 4).
7. Using the piece of the yoke that was cut out in step 5 draw the yoke curve and the neck line curve onto the smocked piece. Using the lines that were just drawn, position the top of the side yoke to the top of the smocked strip. Sew in place with an $^1/_8$" seam (fig. 4).

Embellishing the Sleeves

1. Place marks on the bottom of the sleeve to begin and end smocking design.
2. Run the bottom edge of the sleeve through the pleater placing 6 rows of threads in the bottom of the sleeve. Draw up sleeve to the arm band measurement found in the General Directions on page **.
3. Smock the bottom of the sleeves using the Smocking Sleeve Graph (fig. 5).
4. Block the smocking to the arm band measurement.

Completing the Blouse

1. Referring to the General Blouse Directions II. Neck Finishes, G. Bias Band complete the neck band.
2. Referring to the General Blouse Directions IV. Sleeves to Armholes, attach the sleeves to the bodice.
3. Referring to the General Blouse Directions III. Finishing the Sleeve, E. Cuff with Bias attach the bands to the sleeves. You will not need to gather the lower edge of the sleeves since they are already smocked.

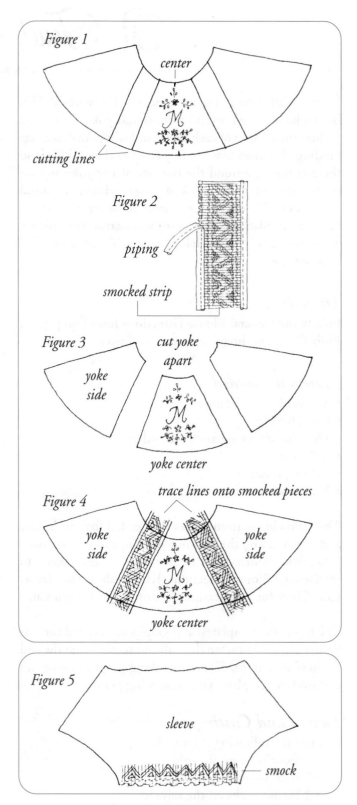

Figure 1 — center — cutting lines

Figure 2 — piping — smocked strip

Figure 3 — cut yoke apart — yoke side — yoke center

Figure 4 — trace lines onto smocked pieces — yoke side — yoke side — yoke center

Figure 5 — sleeve — smock

4. Referring to the General Blouse Directions V. Yoke to Blouse B. Yoke with Piping, attach the yoke to the bodice.
5. Referring to the General Blouse Directions VI. Hemming the Blouse, hem the bottom of the blouse.
6. Referring to the General Blouse Directions VII. Finishing the Back with Buttonholes, finish the back of the blouse.

Sleeve Smocking Graph

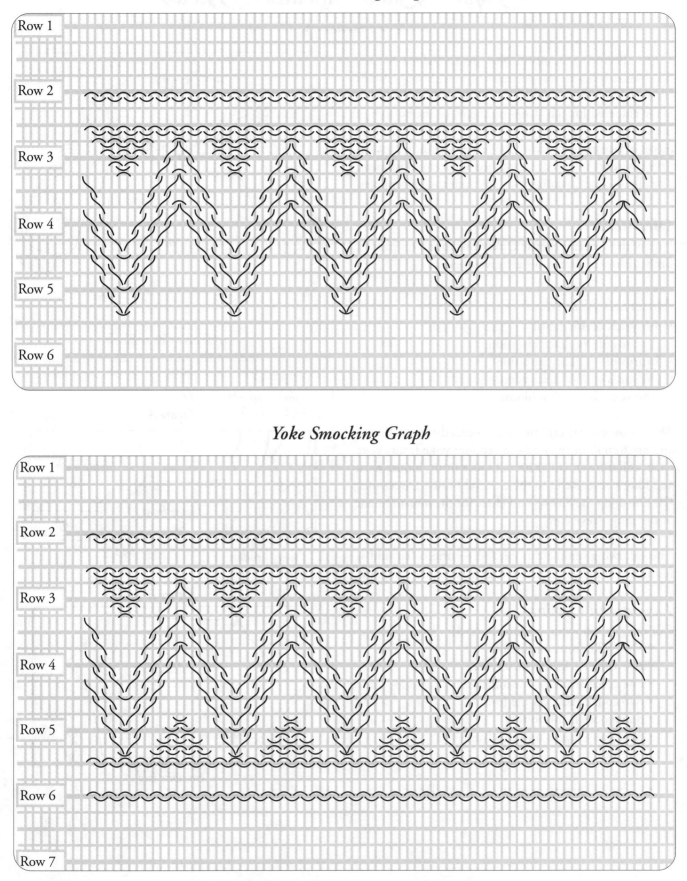

Row 1
Row 2
Row 3
Row 4
Row 5
Row 6

Yoke Smocking Graph

Row 1
Row 2
Row 3
Row 4
Row 5
Row 6
Row 7

Triple Lace Collar Blouse

Featuring beautiful blue Swiss Nelona batiste, this blouse has a round portrait collar with magnificent "triple lace mitered shaping" on the bottom of the collar. Wide gathered French lace is zigzagged to the bottom of the lace shaped insertion treatment. The sleeves have three pieces of lace insertion down the center and the wide cuffs have a piece of the lace edging stitched on for embellishment. The blouse closes in the back with buttons and buttonholes.

Directions

Follow the General Blouse Directions found on page 5. Embellishment directions are given below.

Materials Needed

- 3¼ yards of 45" fabric
- 10 yards of ⅝" Lace insertion
- 5 yards of ⅜" Lace insertion
- 4¾ yards of 2¼" Lace edging
- 6 Buttons for back of blouse

The following pattern pieces are needed for the blouse and are found on the pull-out section: yoke front, yoke back, collar front, collar back, blouse front, blouse back and long sleeve. Refer to the General Blouse Directions, III. Finishing the Sleeve, cuff chart for the measurement of the long sleeve cuff.

The following template is needed for the collar and is found on the pull-out section: Zigzag lace collar template.

Layout and Cutting

Cut out the following (Figures A & B):
- One yoke front on the fold
- two yoke backs on the selvage
- one collar front on the fold
- two collar backs on the fold
- one blouse front on fold
- two blouse backs on the selvage
- two sleeves
- two cuffs
- 1" by 23" bias strip to attach the collar

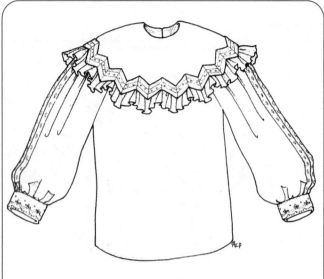

Triple Lace Collar Blouse

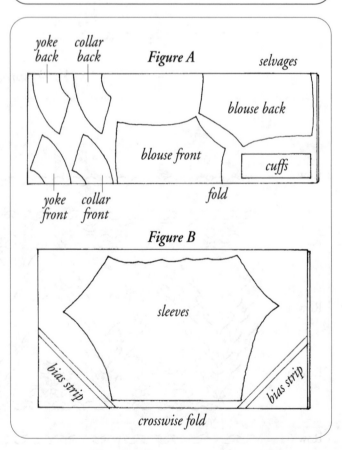

yoke back collar back

Figure A

selvages

blouse back

blouse front

cuffs

fold

yoke front collar front

Figure B

sleeves

bias strip

bias strip

crosswise fold

Embellishing the Collar

1. Sew the shoulder seams of the collar with a $^1/_4$" seam. Finish the seam.
2. Trace the collar template onto collar piece placing the lower points of the template $^1/_4$" from the raw edge of the collar (fig. 1).
3. Cut two pieces of $^5/_8$" lace insertion and one piece of $^3/_8$" lace insertion $3^1/_2$ yards long. Zigzag the strips of lace together using the technique "lace to lace" in the following order: $^5/_8$" lace, $^3/_8$" lace, $^5/_8$" lace (fig. 2).
4. Shape the lace strip around the outer edge of the collar on the lace template line, mitering the lace where needed. Pin the lace in place and zigzag the inside edge of the lace to the collar. Trim the fabric from behind the lace (fig. 3).
5. Gather 4 yards of lace edging to fit the outer edge of the shaped lace and attach the gathered lace to the lace using the technique "lace to lace".
6. On the back edge of the collar turn under $^1/_4$" and $^1/_4$" again and stitch in place to finish the back edge of the fabric and lace (fig. 4).

Embellishing the Sleeves

1. Cut two $^5/_8$" lace strips and one $^3/_8$" lace strip 50" long.
2. Sew the lace together using the technique "lace to lace" in the following order; $^5/_8$" lace $^3/_8$" lace $^5/_8$" lace (fig. 2).
3. Fold each sleeve down the center (this will fall between the middle pleats) and press. Open each sleeve back out.
4. Cut the lace strip in half making two 25" strips.
5. Lay the lace strip on the right side of the sleeve centering the lace strip over the center fold line. Pin in place.
6. Zigzag the outer edges of the lace to the sleeve using the technique "lace to fabric", trim the fabric from behind the lace (fig. 5).

Completing the Blouse

1. Finish the neck edge referring to the General Blouse Directions, II. Neck Finishes, E. Collar.
2. Insert sleeves into armhole referring to the General Blouse Directions, IV. Sleeves to Armholes.
3. Finish the sleeves referring to the General Blouse Directions, III. Finishing the Sleeves, H. Fabric Cuff Covered with Lace.
4. Attach the yoke to the blouse referring to the General Blouse Directions, V. Yoke to Blouse, C. Yoke Seam.
5. Finish the bottom of the blouse referring to the General Blouse Directions, VI. Hemming the Blouse.
6. Finish the back referring to the General Blouse Directions, VII. Finishing the Back with Buttonholes.

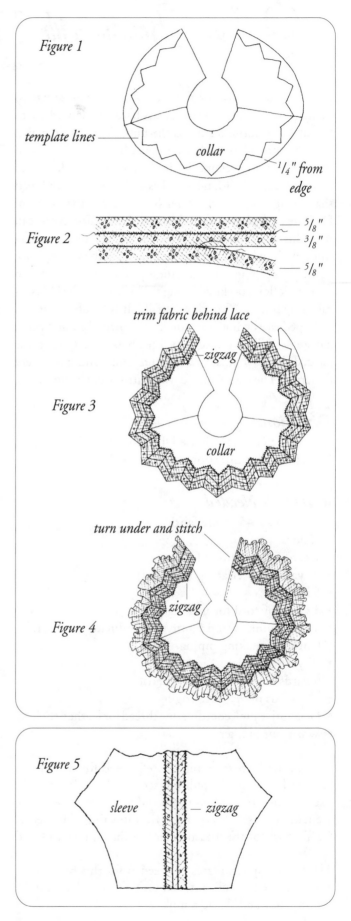

Figure 1

template lines

collar

$^1/_4$" from edge

Figure 2

$^5/_8$"

$^3/_8$"

$^5/_8$"

trim fabric behind lace

zigzag

Figure 3

collar

turn under and stitch

zigzag

Figure 4

Figure 5

sleeve — zigzag

White Batiste with Pink Floral Shadowing

This version of the New Zealand blouse has so many fabulous sewing features it is hard to know where to begin! My favorite feature is the pink floral fabric which shadows through the yoke, the blouse front, the sleeves and the cuffs. The neckline is finished with entredeux and gathered lace. The round yoke has scalloped lace, scalloped shadowing and scalloped featherstitch on the bottom. Delicate pink piping edges the yoke. On the sleeves one can find this same treatment with the floral fabric peeking through the white batiste on the bottom of the sleeve. Once again, pink piping is found at the top of the cuffs, which also have pink floral peeking through. The front of the blouse is called by some a "French waterfall." It is fabulous with its scalloped lace on both sides of the shadowy fabric and white batiste as well as the scalloped featherstitch. I adore the pleated sleeves in this New Zealand blouse and it is so very flattering. The back is closed with buttons and buttonholes.

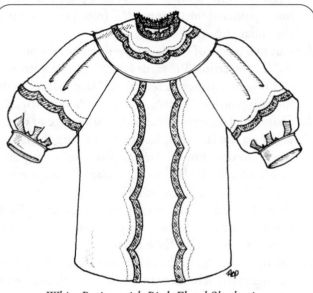

White Batiste with Pink Floral Shadowing

Directions

Follow the General Blouse Directions found on page 5. Embellishment directions are given below.

Materials Needed

- 2⁷/₈ yards - 45" wide fabric
- Nelona
- 1 yard of pink floral fabric
- ¹/₈ yard of interfacing (optional)
- 6 buttons
- 3 yards of cord for making piping
- ¹/₃ yard pink cotton fabric to coordinate with floral fabric for making piping
- ³/₄ yard entredeux
- 6 yards of ⁵/₈" wide lace insertion
- 1¹/₂ yards of ³/₄" lace edging
- Decorative pink coordinating thread for featherstitching
- Wash-out marker

The following pattern pieces are needed for this blouse and are found on the pull-out section: Yoke front, yoke back, blouse front, blouse back and ³/₄ sleeve. Refer to the General Blouse Directions, III. Finishing the Sleeve, Cuff Chart for the measurement of the ³/₄ Length Cuff.

The following templates are needed for this blouse and are found on the pull-out section: Yoke template and the center front and sleeve template.

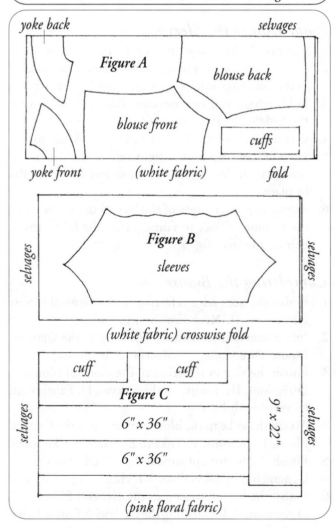

Silk Ribbon Embroidery
and Beading Bows

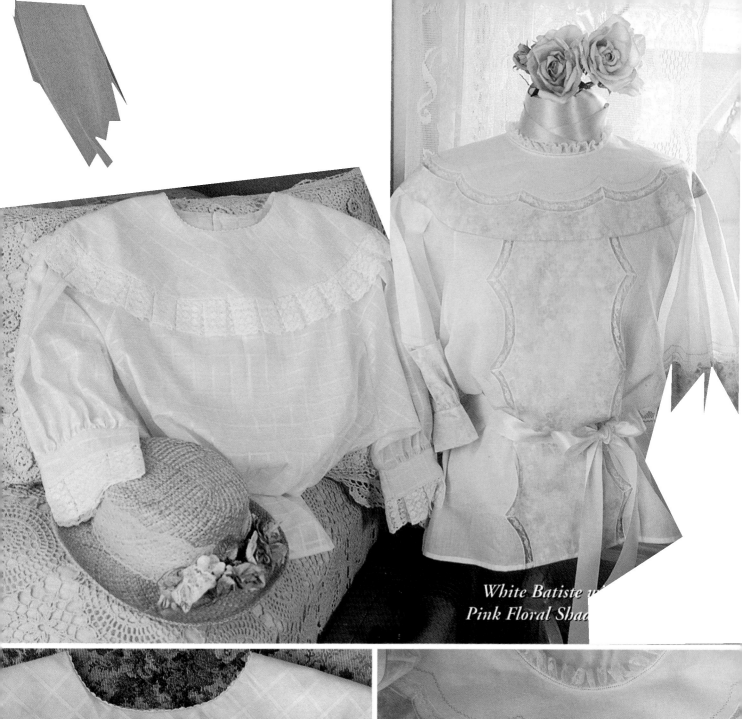

White Batiste with
Pink Floral Shadowing

Detail of Seafoam Lace Blouse

*Detail of White Batiste
with Pink Floral Shadowing*

Silk Ribbon Bows and Flowers

*Detail of Silk Ribbon
Bows and Flowers*

*Detail of Silk Ribbon
Bows and Flowers (Shoulder)*

Beautiful Beaded Bows

Triple Lace Collar Blouse

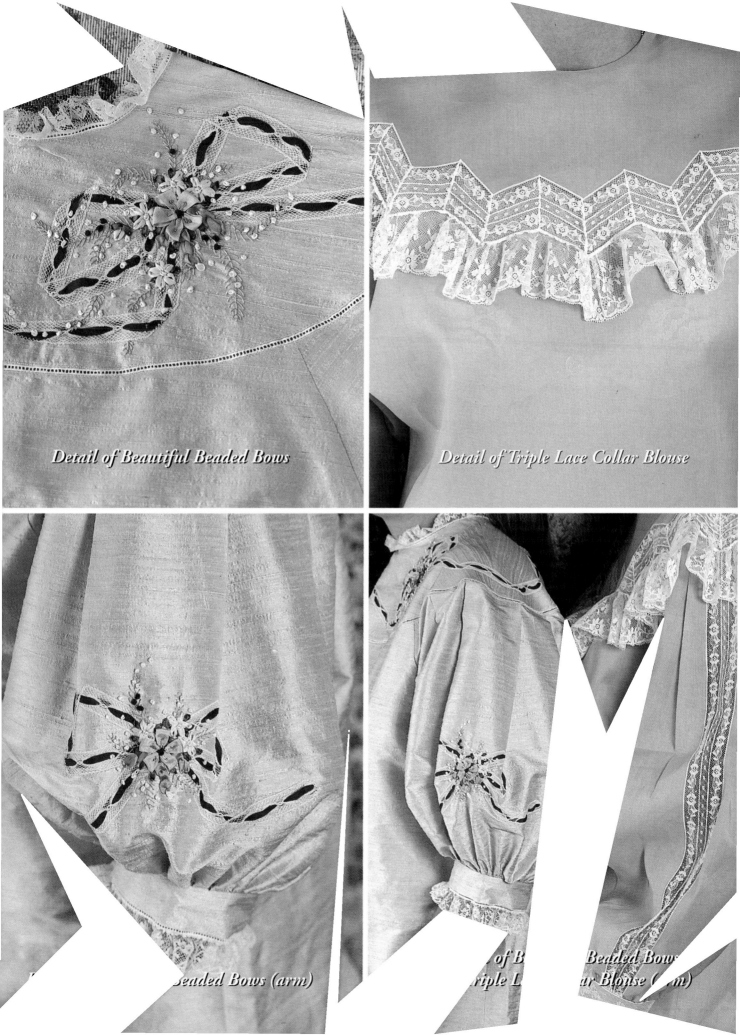

Detail of Beautiful Beaded Bows

Detail of Triple Lace Collar Blouse

Detail of Beautiful Beaded Bows (arm)

Detail of Triple Lace Collar Blouse (arm)

Yellow Linen with Tatting and Crisscross Entredeux

Detail of Yellow Linen with Tatting and Crisscross Entredeux

Detail of Cascading Lace Diamonds

Detail of Yellow Linen with Tatting and Crisscross Entredeux (arm)

Lace Diamond Delight

Creative Cutwork with Tatting

A Touch of Smocking

Detail of Creative Cutwork with Tatting

Detail of A Touch of Smocking

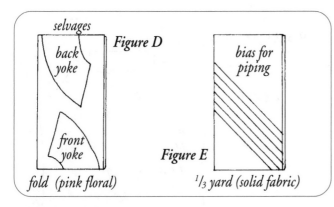

selvages

Figure D

back yoke

front yoke

fold (pink floral)

bias for piping

Figure E

$^{1}/_{3}$ yard (solid fabric)

Layout and Cutting

Cut out the following from the white Nelona: (Figures A & B)
- one yoke front on the fold
- two yoke backs on the selvage
- one blouse front on the fold
- two blouse backs on the selvage
- two $^{3}/_{4}$ sleeves
- two cuffs

Cut out the following from the floral fabric: (Figures C & D)
- one piece of fabric 9" wide by 22" long for the blouse front
- two pieces 36" wide by 6" for sleeves
- one front yoke on the fold
- two back yokes
- two cuffs

Cut out the following from the solid fabric: (Figure E)
- 3 yards of 1" bias for piping (This bias will need to be pieced together to create a continuous length)

Embellishing the Yoke

1. Mark the center front of the blouse and the center of the front yokes and sleeves. Trace the template lines on the sleeves, yokes and blouse front with a wash-out marker (fig. 1).
2. Place the front yoke and the back yokes of the Nelona right sides together and stitch the shoulder seams. Place the front yoke and the back yokes of the floral fabric right sides together and stitch the shoulder seams.
3. Place the floral yoke behind the Nelona yoke with the right side of the floral to the wrong side of the Nelona. Baste along the lower edge of the yoke (fig. 2).
4. Refer to lace shaping techniques and shape the lower edge of the lace insertion along the template line on the yoke. Stitch only the lower edge of the lace with a small zigzag. Trim away the excess floral fabric from behind the lace and upper portion of the yoke (fig. 3).
5. When excess floral fabric is cut away, stitch along the upper edge of the lace insertion with a small zigzag. Trim away the white fabric from behind the lace (fig. 4).

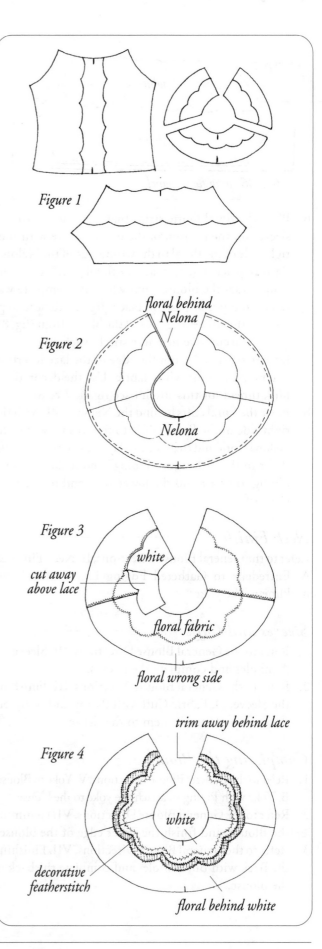

Figure 1

floral behind
Nelona

Figure 2

Nelona

Figure 3

white

cut away above lace

floral fabric

floral wrong side

trim away behind lace

Figure 4

white

decorative featherstitch

floral behind white

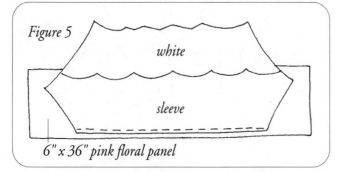

Figure 5

white

sleeve

6" x 36" pink floral panel

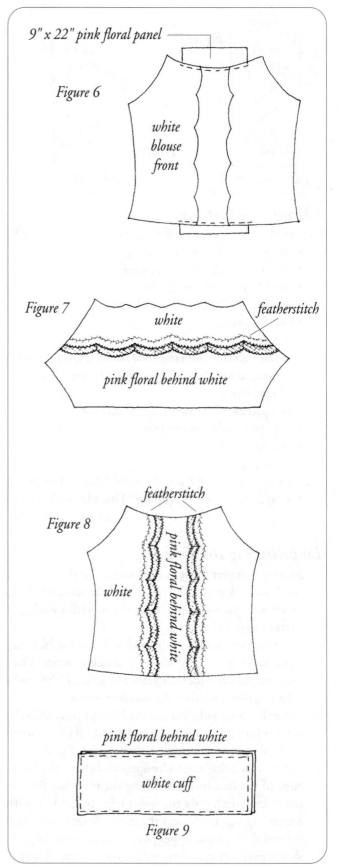

9" x 22" pink floral panel

Figure 6

white
blouse
front

Figure 7

white

featherstitch

pink floral behind white

Figure 8

featherstitch

pink floral behind white

white

pink floral behind white

white cuff

Figure 9

6. Place the floral fabric strips that were cut for the sleeves on the bottom of the blouse sleeve with the right side of the floral to the wrong side of the Nelona. Baste in place (fig. 5). Place the floral panel cut for the front under the blouse front where the template was traced and pin or baste in place (fig. 6). Repeat steps 4 - 5 for the sleeves (fig. 7) and the blouse front (fig. 8).
7. Stitch a decorative machine stitch, such as a featherstitch, $^3/_8$" from the edge of the lace insertion stitching onto the white fabric. Use the decorative pink thread for this stitch (see fig. 4, 7 & 8).
8. Baste the floral cuffs behind the Nelona cuffs with the right side of the floral fabric to the wrong side of the Nelona fabric and treat the two layers as one cuff (fig. 9).
9. Refer to the technique "Piping" and make enough piping to fit around the lower yoke and top edge of the cuffs.

Neck Finish

Refer to the General Blouse Directions, II. Neck Finishes, A. Entredeux to Gathered Edging Lace to finish the neckline of the yoke.

Sleeves and Cuffs

1. Refer to the General Blouse Directions, IV. Sleeves to Armholes and complete the sleeves.
2. Refer to the General Blouse Directions, III. Finishing the Sleeve, D. Fabric Cuff with Piping and complete the cuffs and attach them to the sleeves.

Completing the Blouse

1. Refer to the General Blouse Directions, V. Yoke to Blouse, B. Yoke with Piping to attach the yoke to the blouse.
2. Refer to the General Blouse Directions, VI. Hemming the Blouse, and finish the lower edge of the blouse.
3. Refer to the General Blouse Directions, VII. Finishing the Back with Buttonholes and complete the back of the blouse.

Yellow Linen with Tatting and Crisscrossed Entredeux

Yellow reminds me of sunshine and spring. What a lovely variation of the New Zealand blouse with the crisscrossed machine wing needle diamonds being used on a panel which extends from the neckline to the bottom of the blouse. Entredeux and tiny white tatting finish the neckline. Wide white tatted edging travels around the round yoke in both the front and the back. On either side of the criss-crossed entredeux panel is tatting insertion, feather stitching and a wider row of tatted insertion. This same crisscrossed machine wing needle entredeux treatment is also found on the box pleat on each sleeve, this time with narrow white tatting. The bottom of the sleeves has narrow bias binding with entredeux and flat white tatting on the bottom. The back is closed with buttons and buttonholes.

Directions

Follow the General Blouse Directions found on page 5. Embellishment directions are given below.

Materials Needed

- $2^5/_8$ yards - 45" wide fabric
- 6 buttons
- $4^7/_8$ yards of $3/_8$" tatted insertion
- $2^7/_8$ yards of $3/_4$" tatted insertion
- $1^3/_4$ yards of entredeux
- $2^5/_8$ yards of $1^1/_4$" tatted edging
- $3/_4$ yard of $1/_4$" tatting edging
- Wing needle for pin stitching
- Wash-out marker

The following pattern pieces are needed for this blouse and are found on the pull-out section: Yoke front, yoke back, blouse front, blouse back, short sleeve. Refer to the General Blouse Directions, III. Finishing the Sleeve, Cuff Chart for the measurement of the short sleeve cuff.

The following template is needed for this blouse and is found on the pull-out section: Diamond template for blouse front and sleeve.

Layout and Cutting

Cut out the following: (Figures A & B)
- One yoke front
- two yoke backs
- one blouse front on the fold
- two blouse backs on the selvage
- two short sleeves

Yellow Linen with Tatting and Crisscrossed Entredeux

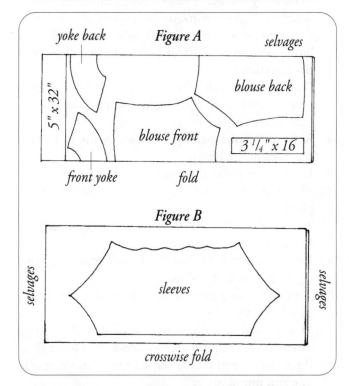

Creating the panels for blouse front and sleeve

1. Cut a rectangle of fabric 5" wide by 32" long for the front blouse panel and two rectangles $3^1/_4$" wide by 16" long for the sleeve.
2. Trace the diamond template onto the rectangles repositioning the template until all of the rectangles are covered. Be sure to line the template up square on the fabric.

3. Referring to the section on Machine Entredeux stitch along the drawn lines using a wing needle (fig. 1).

4. Refer to the technique "extra-stable lace finish" and attach the $^3/_8$" tatting insertion along the two long sides of the panel for the blouse front and along the two long sides of each of the panels for the sleeves. The finished width of the blouse panel will be $4^1/_4$" of fabric or total of 5" with the tatting on both sides. The finished width of the sleeve panels will be $2^1/_2$" wide of fabric or a total of $3^1/_4$" with the tatting on both sides (fig. 2).

5. Lay these panels aside to be inserted into the blouse front and sleeves.

Constructing the Blouse

1. Draw a line down the center of each sleeve.
2. Place the panels with the entredeux stitching and tatting down the center of each sleeve.
3. Refer to the technique "extra-stable lace finish" and attach the panel to each sleeve.
4. Trim away the excess panel even with the top and bottom of the sleeve (fig. 3).
5. Trim away the sleeve fabric from behind the panel.
6. Refer to IV. Sleeves to Armholes, and attach the sleeves to the blouse. Adjust the pleats so that the fold lines of the center pleat fall just to the outside edge of the insertion.
7. Place the front yoke and the back yokes right sides together and stitch the shoulder seams. Mark the center front of the yoke.
8. Refer to V. Yoke to Blouse, C. Yoke Seam, and attach the yoke to the blouse.
9. Draw a line down the center front of the blouse.
10. Place the panel down the center front and pin in place.
11. Trace the neckline of the blouse and the lower edge of the blouse onto the panel.
12. Refer to "extra-stable lace finish" and attach the panel to the center of the blouse.
13. Trim away the excess blouse fabric from behind the panel (fig. 4).
14. Measure over from the outside edge of the 3/8" tatted insertion $^1/_2$" and draw a line down the blouse.
15. Place the edge of the $^3/_4$" tatted insertion along this line and pin in place.
16. Place the wide tatted edging along the seam line of the yoke attaching it with a tiny zigzag. The end of the wide edging will be underneath the $^3/_4$" tatted insertion (fig. 4).
17. Refer to the technique for "extra-stable lace finish" and attach the insertion to the blouse.
18. Trim away the fabric behind the tatted insertion.

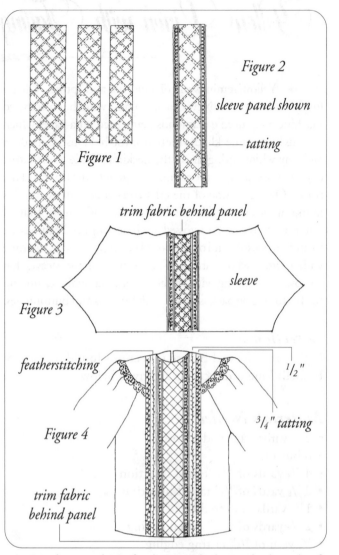

Figure 1

Figure 2

sleeve panel shown

— tatting

trim fabric behind panel

Figure 3

sleeve

featherstitching

Figure 4

$^1/_2$"

$^3/_4$" tatting

trim fabric behind panel

19. Stitch a machine feather stitch down the length of the blouse in the space of fabric between the two insertions (fig. 4).

Neck Finish

Refer to the General Blouse Directions, II. Neck Finishes, B. Entredeux to Flat Lace, treating the tatted edging as lace, and complete the neckline of the yoke.

Sleeves and Cuffs

1. Refer to the General Blouse Directions, III. Finishing the Sleeve, F. Cuff With Bias, and Entredeux and Flat Edging or Tatting complete the lower edge of the sleeve.

Completing the Blouse

1. Refer to the General Blouse Directions, VI. Hemming the Blouse, and finish the lower edge of the blouse.
2. Refer to General Directions, VII. Finishing the Back with Buttonholes and complete the back of the blouse.

Beginning French Sewing Techniques

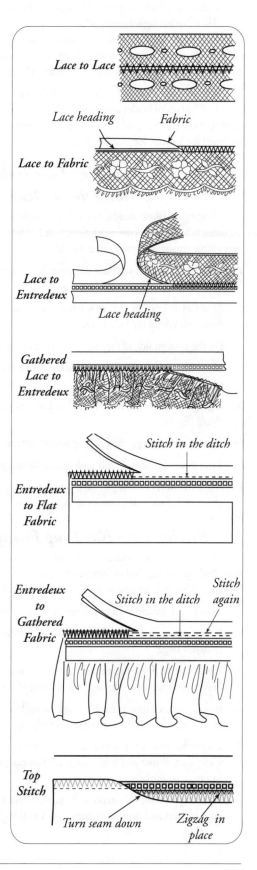

Lace to Lace

Butt together and zigzag.

Suggested machine settings: Width $2^1/2$, length 1.

Lace to Fabric

Place right sides together.

Fabric extends $1/8$" from lace.

Zigzag off the edge and over the heading of the lace.

Suggested Machine Settings: Width $3^1/2$, Length $1/2$ to 1 (almost a satin stitch).

Lace to Entredeux

Trim batiste from one side of the entredeux.

Butt lace to entredeux and zigzag.

Suggested Machine Settings: Width $2^1/2$, Length $1^1/2$.

Gathered Lace to Entredeux

Trim one side of the entredeux.

Gather lace by pulling heading thread.

Butt together and zigzag.

Suggested Machine Settings: Width $2^1/2$, Length $1^1/2$.

Entredeux to Flat Fabric

Place fabric to entredeux, right sides together.

Stitch in the ditch with a regular straight stitch.

Trim seam allowance to $1/8$".

Zigzag over the seam allowance.

Suggested Machine Settings: Width $2^1/2$, Length $1^1/2$.

Entredeux to Gathered Fabric

Gather fabric using two gathering rows.

Place gathered fabric to entredeux, right sides together.

Stitch in the ditch with a regular straight stitch.

Stitch again $1/16$" away from the first stitching.

Trim seam allowance to $1/8$".

Zigzag over the seam allowance.

Suggested Machine Settings: Width $2^1/2$, Length $1^1/2$.

Top Stitch

Turn seam down, away from the lace, entredeux, etc.

Tack in place using a zigzag.

Suggested Machine Settings: Width $1^1/2$, Length $1^1/2$.

Cutting Fabric From Behind Lace That Has Been Shaped and Zigzagged

I absolutely love two pairs of Fiskars Scissors for the tricky job of cutting fabric from behind lace that has been shaped and stitched on. The first is Fiskars 9491, blunt tip 5" scissors. They look much like kindergarten scissors because of the blunt tips; however, they are very sharp. They cut fabric away from behind laces with ease. By the way, both of the scissors mentioned in this section are made for either right handed or left handed people.

The second pair that I really love for this task is the Fiskars 9808 curved blade craft scissors. The curved blades are very easy to use when working in tricky, small areas of lace shaping. Fiskars are crafted out of permanent stainless steel and are precision ground and hardened for a sharp, long lasting edge.

Repairing Lace Holes Which You Didn't Mean To Cut!

Trimming fabric away from behind stitched-down lace can be difficult. It is not uncommon to slip, thus cutting a hole in your lace work. How do you repair this lace with the least visible repair? It is really quite simple.

1. Look at the pattern in the lace where you have cut the hole. Is it in a flower, in a dot series, or in the netting part of the lace (fig. 1)?

2. After you identify the pattern where the hole was cut, cut another piece of lace ¹/₄" longer than each side of the hole in the lace.

3. On the bottom side of the lace in the garment, place the lace patch (fig. 2).

4. Match the design of the patch with the design of the lace around the hole where it was cut.

5. Zigzag around the cut edges of the lace hole, trying to catch the edges of the hole in your zigzag (fig 3).

6. Now, you have a patched and zigzagged pattern.

7. Trim away the leftover ends underneath the lace you have just patched (fig. 3).

8. And don't worry about a piece of patched lace. My grandmother used to say, "Don't worry about that. You'll never notice it on a galloping horse."

Piecing Lace Not Long Enough For Your Needs

From my sewing experience, sometimes you will need a longer piece of lace than you have. Perhaps you cut the lace incorrectly or bought less than you needed and had to go back for more. Whatever the reason, if you need to make a lace strip longer, it is easy to do.

1. Match your pattern with two strips that will be joined later (figs. 1 and 3).

2. Is your pattern a definite flower? Is it a definite diamond or some other pattern that is relatively large?

3. If you have a definite design in the pattern, you can join pieces by zigzagging around that design and then down through the heading of the lace (fig. 2).

4. If your pattern is tiny, you can zigzag at an angle joining the two pieces (fig. 2). Trim away excess laces close to the zigzagged seam (fig. 4).

5. Forget that you have patched laces and complete the dress. If you discover that the lace is too short before you begin stitching, you can plan to place the pieced section in an inconspicuous place.

6. If you were already into making the garment when you discovered the short lace, simply join the laces and continue stitching as if nothing had happened.

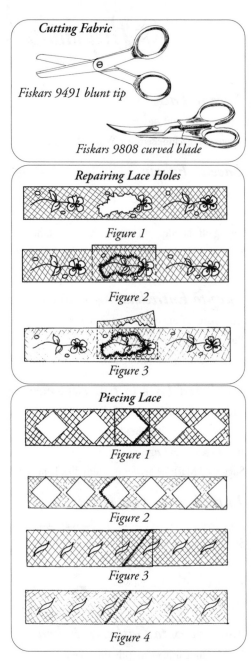

Cutting Fabric

Fiskars 9491 blunt tip

Fiskars 9808 curved blade

Repairing Lace Holes

Figure 1

Figure 2

Figure 3

Piecing Lace

Figure 1

Figure 2

Figure 3

Figure 4

If Your Fancy Band Is Too Short

Not to worry; cut down the width of your skirt. Always make your skirt adapt to your lace shapes, not the lace shapes to your skirt.

Making Diamonds, Hearts, Tear-Drops, Or Circles Fit Skirt Bottom

How do you make sure that you engineer your diamonds, hearts, teardrops, or circles to exactly fit the width skirt that you are planning? The good news is that you don't. Make your shapes any size that you want. Stitch them onto your skirt, front and back, and cut away the excess skirt width. Or, you can stitch up one side seam, and zigzag your shapes onto the skirt, and cut away the excess on the other side before you make your other side seam.

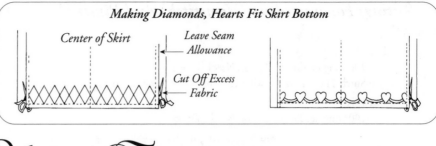

Making Diamonds, Hearts Fit Skirt Bottom

Center of Skirt — Leave Seam Allowance — Cut Off Excess Fabric

Machine Entredeux

Making Entredeux (Or Hemstitching) On Today's Computer Sewing Machines

About eight years ago I was conned into purchasing a 1905 hemstitching machine for $1500. I was told that it had a perfect stitch and that stitch (about 2 inches) was demonstrated to me by the traveling salesman. I was very happy to finally have one of those wonderful machines. Guess how long that wonderful machine lasted before it broke down? I stitched about 10 inches more which looked great; at that point, the stitching was awful. I called several repairmen. It never made a decent hemstitch again.

The good news to follow this sad story is that today's new computer machines do an excellent job of making hemstitching and they work! I am going to give our favorite settings for our favorite sewing machines. Before you buy a new sewing machine, if you love heirloom sewing, please go try out each of these machines and see if you love these stitches as much as we do.

Using A Stabilizer With Wing Needle Hemstitching Or Pinstitching

Before you do any hemstitching or any decorative work with a wing needle which involves lots of stitching on these wonderful machines, first let me tell you that **you must use a stabilizer**! You can use stitch-n-tear, computer paper, tissue paper (not quite strong enough but o.k. in certain situations), wax paper, physician's examining table paper, typing paper, adding machine paper or almost any other type of paper. When you are doing heavy stitching such as a feather stitch, I recommend the type of paper which physicians spread out over their examining tables. You can get a roll of it at any medical supply place. If you use stitch-n-tear or adding machine paper in feather stitch type stitches, it is difficult to pull away all of the little pieces which remain when you take the paper from the back of the garment. This physician's paper seems to tear away pretty easily.

Preparing Fabric Before Beginning Hemstitching or Pinstitching

Stiffen fabric with spray starch before lace shaping or decorative stitching with the hemstitches and wing needles. Use a hair dryer to dry the lace before you iron it if you have spray starched it too much. Also, if you wet your fabrics and laces too much with spray starch, place a piece of tissue paper on top of your work, and dry iron it dry. Hemstitching works best on natural fibers such as linen, cotton, cotton batiste, silk or cotton organdy. I don't advise

hemstitching a fabric with a high polyester content. Polyester has a memory. If you punch a hole in polyester, it remembers the original positioning of the fibers, and the hole wants to close up.

Threads To Use For Pinstitching Or Hemstitching

Use all cotton thread, 50, 60, 70 or 80 weight. If you have a thread breaking problem, you can also use a high quality polyester thread or a cotton covered polyester thread, like the Coats and Clark for machine lingerie and embroidery. Personally, I like to press needle down on all of the entredeux and pin stitch settings.

Pinstitching Or Point de Paris Stitch With A Sewing Machine

The pin stitch is another lovely "entredeux look" on my favorite machines. It is a little more delicate. Pin stitch looks similar to a ladder with **one of the long sides of the ladder missing**. Imagine the steps being fingers which reach over into the actual lace piece to grab the lace. The side of the ladder, the long side, will be stitched on the fabric right along side of the outside of the heading of the lace. The fingers reach into the lace to grab it. You need to look on all of the pinstitch settings given below and realize that you have to use reverse image on one of the sides of lace so that the fingers will grab into the lace while the straight side goes on the outside of the lace heading.

Settings For Entredeux (Hemstitch) And Pinstitch

Pfaff 7570

Pinstitch

-100 wing needle, A - 2 Foot, Needle Down
-Stitch 112, tension 3, twin needle button, 4.0 width, 3.0 length

Entredeux

-100 wing needle, A - 2 Foot, Needle Down

	width	length
Stitch #132	3.5	5.0
Stitch #113	4.0	2.0
Stitch #114	3.5	2.5
Stitch #115	3.5	3.0

Bernina 1630

Pinstitch

- 100 wing needle
- 1630 menu G, Pattern #10, SW - 2.5, SL - 2

Entredeux

- 100 wing needle
- 1630 menu G, pattern #5, SW - 3.5, SL - 3

Viking#1+

Pinstitch

- 100 wing needle
- Stitch D6, width 2.5-3; length 2.5-3

Entredeux

- 100 wing needle
- Stitch D7 (width and length are already set in)

Elna 9000 and DIVA

Pinstitch

- 100 wing needle
- Stitch #120 (length and width are already set in)

Entredeux

- 100 wing needle
- Stitch #121 (length and width are already set)

Singer XL - 100

Pinstitch

- 100 Wing Needle
- Screen #3
- Stitch #7
- Width 4 (length changes with width)

Entredeux

- 100 Wing needle
- Screen #3
- Stitch #8
- Width 5 (Medium) or 4 (small)

New Home 9000

Pinstitch

- 100 Wing Needle
- Stitch #26 (width 2.5; length 2.5)

Hemstitch

- 100 wing needle
- Stitch #39 (width 4.0; length 1.5)

Esanté - Baby Lock

Choose Decorative Stitch-Heirloom

Pinstitch

- 100 wing needle
- Stitch #4

Hemstitch

- 100 wing needle
- Stitch #5

Attaching Shaped Lace To The Garment With Machine Entredeux Or Pinstitching And A Wing Needle

Probably my favorite place to use the machine entredeux/wing needle hemstitching is to attach shaped laces to a garment. Simply shape your laces in the desired shapes such as hearts, diamonds, ovals, loops, circles, or bows, and stitch the stitch. In addition to stitching this gorgeous decorative stitch, it also attaches the shaped lace to the garment (fig. 1). Always use stabilizer when using this type of heavy hemstitching.

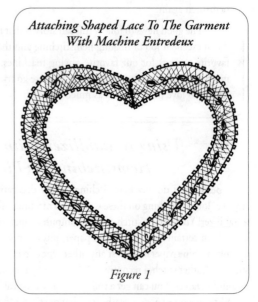

Attaching Shaped Lace To The Garment With Machine Entredeux

Figure 1

Gathering The Puffing Using The Gathering Foot On Your Machine

Two years ago, I wouldn't have told you that this was the easiest method of applying puffing into a round portrait collar. The reason being I didn't know how to make perfect puffing using the gathering foot for the sewing machine. I thought you used the edge of the gathering foot to guide the fabric underneath the gathering foot. This left about a ¹/₄" seam allowance. It also made the gathers not perfect in some places with little "humps" and unevenness on some portions. Therefore, I wasn't happy with puffing made on the gathering foot. When I asked my friend, Sue Hausman, what might be wrong, she explained to me that to make perfect gathering, you had to move the fabric over so that you would have at least a ¹/₂" seam allowance. She further explained that there are two sides to the feed dogs; when you use the side of the gathering foot, then the fabric only catches on one side of the feed dogs. It works like magic to move your fabric over and guide it along one of the guide lines on the sewing machine. If your machine doesn't have these lines, simply put a piece of tape down to make a proper guide line.

Making Puffing with a Gathering Foot

1. The speed of the sewing needs to be consistent. Sew either fast or slow but do not sew fast then slow then fast again. For the beginner, touch the "sew slow" button (if available on your machine). This will help to keep a constant speed.

2. The puffing strip should be gathered with a ¹/₂ seam allowance, with an approximate straight stitch length of 4, right side up (fig. 1). Remember that you can adjust your stitch length to make your puffing looser or fuller. Do not let the strings of the fabric wrap around the foot of the machine. This will cause to fabric to back up behind the foot causing an uneven seam allowance, as well as uneven gathers. Leave the thread tails long in case adjustments are needed. One side of the gathering is now complete (fig. 2).

3. Begin gathering the second side of the strip, right side up. This row of gathering will be made from the bottom of the strip to the top of the strip. In other words, bi-directional sewing (first side sewn from the top to the bottom, second side sewn from the bottom to the top) is allowed. Gently unfold the ruffle with the left hand allowing flat fabric to feed under the foot. Do not apply any pressure to the fabric (fig. 3). The feeding must remain constant. Leave the thread tails long in case adjustments are needed. The puffing strip in now complete.

Placing Machine Gathered Puffing Into A Collar

1. Cut your strips of fabric.

2. Gather both sides of the puffing, running the fabric under the gathering foot. Be sure you have at least a ¹/₂" seam allowance. When you use a gathering foot, the mobility of the puffing isn't as great as when you gather it the other way.

3. You, of course, have two raw edges when you gather puffing with the gathering foot (fig. 1).

4. Shape the puffing around the fabric board below the row of lace (or rows of lace) that you have already shaped into the rounded shape. Place the pins into the board through the outside edge of the puffing. Place the pins right into the place where the gathering row runs in the fabric (fig. 2).

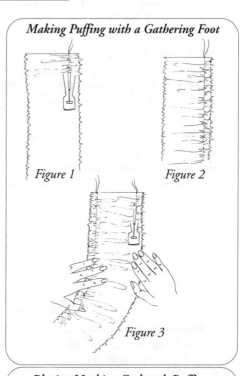

Making Puffing with a Gathering Foot

Figure 1

Figure 2

Figure 3

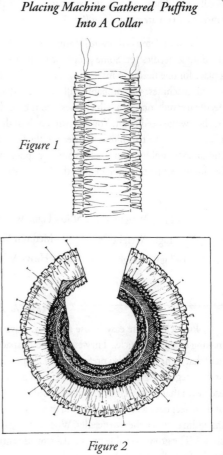

Placing Machine Gathered Puffing Into A Collar

Figure 1

Figure 2

5. Pull the raw edge of the machine puffed strip up underneath the finished edge of the curved lace, so that your zigzagging to attach the puffing will be on the machine gathering line. Put the rounded lace edge on top of the puffing. Pin the bottom edge of the puffing first so you can "arrange" the top fullness underneath the curved lace edge which is already in place (the top piece of lace) (see fig. 2).

6. It will be necessary to "sort of" arrange the machine gathered puffing, especially on the top edge which will be gathered the fullest on your collar, and pin it where you want it since the machine gathering thread doesn't give too much. After you have pinned and poked the gathering into place where it looks pretty on the top and the bottom, flat pin it to the tissue paper and zigzag the puffing strip to the lace, stitching right on top of the lace.

NOTE: You will have an unfinished fabric edge underneath the place where you stitched the lace to the puffing. That is okay. After you have zigzagged the puffing to the lace, then trim away the excess fabric underneath the lace edge. Be careful, of course, when you trim this excess fabric, not to accidentally cut the lace.

7. If you have a machine entredeux/wing needle option on your sewing machine, you can stitch this beautiful stitch in place of the zigzagging. Since the fabric is gathered underneath the lace, you will have to be very careful stitching to get a pretty stitch.

8. Shape another piece of lace around the bottom of this puffing, bringing the inside piece of curved lace exactly to fit on top of the gathering line in the puffing. Once again, you will have unfinished fabric underneath the place where you will zigzag the lace to the puffing collar. After zigzagging the lace to the puffing collar, trim the excess fabric away.

9. Continue curving the rest of the laces to make the collar as wide as you want it to be.

Basic Pintucking

Double Needles

Double needles come in different sizes. The first number on the double needle is the distance between the needles. The second number on the needle is the actual size of the needle. The chart below shows some of the double needle sizes. The size needle that you choose will depend on the weight of the fabric that you are pintucking (fig. 1).

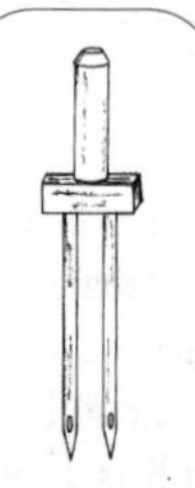

Figure 1

Let me relate a little more information for any of you who haven't used the double needles yet. Some people have said to me, "Martha, I only have a place for one needle in my sewing machine." That is correct and on most sewing machines, you probably still can use a double needle. The double needle has only one stem which goes into the needle slot; the double needles join on a little bar below the needle slot. You use two spools of thread when you thread the double needles. If you don't have two spools of thread of the fine thread which you use for pintucking, then run an extra bobbin and use it as another spool of thread. For most shaped pintucking on heirloom garments, I prefer either the 1.6/70, the 1.6/80 or the 2.0/80 size needle.

a. 1.6/70 - Light Weight   d. 2.5/80 - Light Weight
b. 1.6/80 - Light Weight   e. 3.0/90 - Medium Weight
c. 2.0/80 - Light Weight   f. 4.0/100 - Heavy Weight

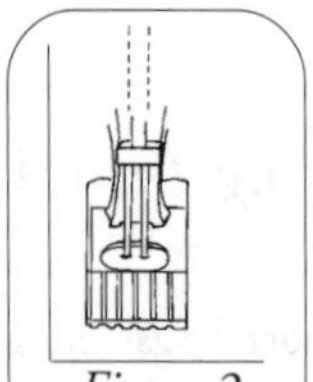

Figure 2

Pintuck Feet

Pintuck feet are easy to use and they shave hours off pintucking time when you are making straight pintucks. They enable you to space straight pintucks perfectly. I might add here that some people also prefer a pintuck foot when making curved and angled pintucks. I prefer a regular zigzag sewing foot for curved pintucks. Pintuck feet correspond to the needle used with that pintuck foot; the needle used corresponds to the weight of fabric. The bottom of these feet have a certain number of grooves 3, 5, 7, or 9. The width of the groove matches the width between the two needles. When making straight pintucks, use a pintuck foot of your choice. The grooves enable one to make those pintucks as close or as far away as the distance on the foot allows (fig. 2).

Preparing Fabric For Pintucking

Do I spray starch the fabric before I pintuck it? I usually do not spray starch fabric before pintucking it. Always press all-cotton fabric. A polyester/cotton blend won't need to be pressed unless it is very wrinkled. Tucks tend to lay flatter if you stiffen fabric with spray starch first; that is why I don't advise spray starching the fabric first in most cases. Pintuck a small piece of your chosen fabric with starch and one without starch, then make your own decision.

Straight Pintucking With A Pintuck Foot

Some of my favorite places for straight pintucks are on high yoke bodices of a dress and along the sleeves. On ladies blouses, straight pintucks are lovely running vertically on the front and back of the blouse, and so slenderizing! One of the prettiest treatments of straight pintucks on ladies blouses is stitching about three to five pintucks right down the center back of the blouse. Tuck a little shaped bow or heart on the center back of the blouse; stitch several tiny pintucks and top them off with a lace shape in the center back. Horizontally placed straight pintucks are lovely running across the back yoke of a tailored blouse. Tucks are always pretty running around the cuff of a blouse. I love pintucks just about anywhere.

1. Insert your double needle. Thread machine with two spools of thread. Thread one spool at a time (including the needle). This will help keep the threads from becoming twisted while stitching the tucks. This would be a good time to look in the guide book which came with your sewing machine for directions on using pintuck feet and double needles. Some sewing machines have a special way of threading for use with double needles.

2. The first tuck must be straight. To make this first tuck straight, do one of three things: (a.) Pull a thread all the way across the fabric and follow along that pulled line. (b.) Using a measuring stick, mark a straight line along the fabric. Stitch on that line. (c.) Fold the fabric in half and press that fold. Stitch along that folded line.

3. Place the fabric under the foot for the first tuck and straight stitch the desired length of pintuck. (Length=1 to $2^1/_2$; Needle position is center) (fig. 1).

4. Place your first tuck into one of the grooves in your pintuck foot. The space between each pintuck depends on the placement of the first pintuck (fig. 2).

5. Continue pintucking by placing the last pintuck made into a groove in the foot.

Straight Pintucking Without A Pintuck Foot

1. Use a double needle. Use your regular zigzag foot.

2. Thread your double needles.

3. Draw the first line of pintucking. Pintuck along that line. At this point you can use the edge of your presser foot as a guide (fig. 3).

NOTE: You might find a "generic" pintuck foot for your particular brand of machine.

Corded Pintucks

Cords make pintucks more prominent. Use Mettler gimp or #8 pearl cotton. Cording comes in handy when pintucks are being shaped. When pintucking across a bias with a double needle, you may get some distortion. The cord acts as a filler and will keep the fabric from distorting. Sometimes you might choose to use cording in order to add color to your pintucks. If you asked me, "Martha, do you usually cord pintucks?," my answer would be "no." However, just because I don't usually cord pintucks, doesn't mean that you won't prefer to cord them.

Some machines have a little device which sits in the base of the machine and sticks up just a little bit. That device tends to make the pintucks stand up a little more for a higher raised effect. Some people really like this feature.

1. If your machine has a hole in the throat plate, run the cord up through that hole and it will be properly placed without another thought (fig. 1).

2. If your machine does not have a hole in the throat plate, put the gimp or pearl cotton underneath the fabric, lining it up with the pintuck groove. Once you get the cording lined up under the proper groove, it will follow along for the whole pintuck (fig. 2).

3. You can stitch pintucks without a pintuck foot at all. Some sewing machines have a foot with a little hole right in the middle of the foot underneath the foot. That is a perfectly proper place to place the cord for shadow pintucks. Remember, if you use a regular foot for pintucking, you must use the side of the foot for guiding your next pintuck.

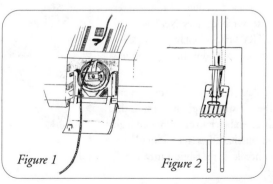

Figure 1   Figure 2

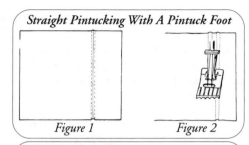

Straight Pintucking With A Pintuck Foot

Figure 1   Figure 2

Straight Pintucking Without A Pintuck Foot

Figure 3

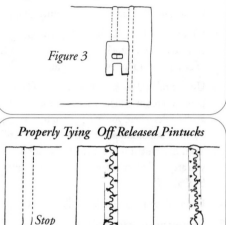

Properly Tying Off Released Pintucks

Stop

Figure 1   Figure 2   Figure 3

Shaping Curves And Angles With Pintucks

Pintucks are inexpensive to make. They add texture and dimension without adding cost to the dress. They're rarely found on store-bought clothing. One of my favorite things in the whole world to do is to follow lace shapes with pintucks or decorative stitches on my machine for an enchanting finish. Or you may simply use your template and pintuck the shape instead of using lace. For threads, use white-on-white, ecru-on-ecru, or any pastel color on white or ecru.

The effect of shaped pintucks is so fabulous and so interesting. Virtually everyone is afraid that they don't know how to make those fabulous pintucks that transform a garment into a pintuck fantasy. It is so easy that I just can't wait to share with you the tricks. I promise, nobody in my schools all over the world ever believes me when I tell them this easy way. Then, everybody, virtually everybody, has done these curved and angled pintucks with absolute perfection. They usually say, "This is really magic!"

The big question here is, "What foot do I use for scalloped pintucks?" For straight pintucks, I use a pintuck foot with the grooves. That foot is fine for curved or scalloped pintucks also, but I prefer either the regular zigzag foot or the clear appliqué foot, which is plastic and allows easy "see through" of the turning points. Try your pintuck foot, your regular sewing foot, and your clear appliqué foot to see which one you like the best. Like all aspects of heirloom sewing, the "best" foot is really your personal preference. Listed below are my absolute recommendations for curved and angled pintucks.

Martha's General Rules Of Curving And Angling Pintucks

1. Use a regular zigzag foot, or a pintuck foot (fig. 1).

2. Either draw on your pintuck shape, or zigzag your lace insertion to the garment. You can either draw on pintuck shapes or follow your lace shaping. My favorite way to make lots of pintucks is to follow lace shaping which has already been stitched to the garment.

3. Using a ruler, draw straight lines with a fabric marker or washable pencil, bisecting each point where you will have to turn around with your pintuck. In other words, draw a line at all angles where you will have to turn your pintuck in order to keep stitching. This is the most important point to make with curved and angled pintucks. When you are going around curves, this bi-secting line is not necessary since you don't stop and pivot when you are turning curves. Everywhere you have to stop and pivot, these straight lines must be drawn (fig. 2).

4. Use a 1.6 or a 2.0 double needle. Any wider doesn't curve or turn well!

5. Set your machine for straight sewing, L=1.5. Notice this is a very short stitch. When you turn angles, this short stitch is necessary for pretty turns.

6. Press "Needle Down" on your sewing machine if your machine has this feature. This means that when you stop sewing at any time, your needle will remain in the fabric.

7. Stitch, using either the first line you drew or following around the lace shaping which you have already stitched to your garment. The edge of your presser foot will guide along the outside of the lace shape. When you go around curves, turn your fabric and keep stitching. Do not pick up your foot and pivot, this makes the curves jumpy, not smooth (fig. 3).

8. When you come to a pivot point, let your foot continue to travel until you can look into the hole of the foot, and see that your double needles have straddled the line you drew on the fabric. Remember your needles are in the fabric (fig. 4).

9. Sometimes, the needles won't exactly straddle the line exactly the way they straddled the line on the last turn around. Lift the presser foot. (Remember, you needles are still in the fabric.) Turn your fabric where the edge of the presser foot properly begins in a new direction following your lace insertion lace shaping or your drawn line, lower the presser foot, and begin sewing again (fig. 5).

10. Wait A Minute! Most of you are now thinking, "Martha, You Are Crazy. There are two major problems with what you just said. You said to leave the double needles in the fabric, lift the presser foot , turn the fabric, lower the presser foot and begin sewing again. If I do that I will probably break my double needles, and there will be a big wad or hump of fabric where I twisted the fabric to turn around to go in a new direction. That will never work!" I know you are thinking these two things because everybody does. Neither one of these things will happen! It is really just like MAGIC. TRY THIS TECHNIQUE AND SEE WHAT I AM SAYING. Ladies all over the world absolutely adore this method and nobody believes how easy it is.

11. After you get your first row of double needle pintucks, then you can use the edge of your regular zigzag sewing machine foot, guiding along the just stitched pintuck row as the guide point for more rows. The only thing you have to remember, is to make long enough lines to bisect each angle that you are going to turn. You must have these turn-around lines drawn so you can know where to stop sewing, leave the needles in the fabric, turn around, and begin stitching again. These lines are the real key.

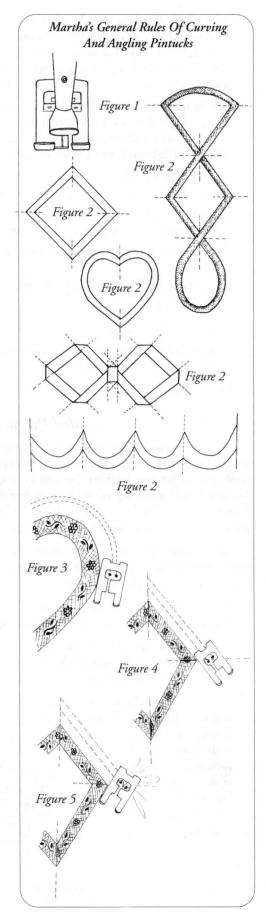

Martha's General Rules Of Curving And Angling Pintucks

Figure 1

Figure 2

Figure 2

Figure 2

Figure 2

Figure 2

Figure 3

Figure 4

Figure 5

Lace Shaping Techniques

General Lace Shaping Supplies

- ❁ Fabric to apply lace shape
- ❁ Lace (usually insertion lace)
- ❁ Glass head pins
- ❁ Spray starch
- ❁ Lightweight sewing thread

- ❁ Lace shaping board or covered cardboard
- ❁ Washout marker or washout pencil
- ❁ Wing needle (optional)
- ❁ Stabilizer (If a wing needle stitch is used)

Tracing the Template

Trace the template on the fabric with a wash out marker. Margaret Boyles taught me years ago that it is simpler to draw your shapes on fabric by making dots about one half inch apart than it is to draw a solid line. This also means less pencil or marker to get out of the fabric when your lace shaping is finished. Mark

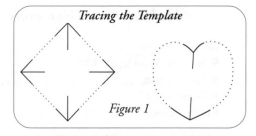

Tracing the Template

Figure 1

all angles with miter lines (a line dividing the angle in half). Sometimes it is helpful to make the solid lines at the angles and miter lines (**fig. 1**). Hint: If you do not want to draw the template on the fabric, trace the template on stabilizer or paper with a permanent marker. Place the template under the fabric. Because the fabric is "see-through" the lines can be seen clearly. Shape the lace along the template lines. Complete the design as stated in the lace shaping directions. Remember to remove the template paper before stitching so that the permanent pen lines are not caught in the stitching.

Using Glass Head Pins

Purchasing GLASS HEAD PINS is one of the first and most critical steps to lace shaping. All types of lace shaping must be pinned in place, starched lightly and pressed. The iron is placed directly on top of the pins. Since plastic head pins melt onto your fabric and ruin your project, obviously they won't do. Metal pins such as the iris pins with the skinny little metal heads won't melt; however, when you pin hundreds of these little pins into the lace shaping board, your finger will have one heck of a hole poked into it. Please purchase glass head pins and throw away your plastic head pins. Glass head pins can be purchased by the box or by the card. For dress projects, as many 100 pins might be needed for each section of lace shaping. So, make sure to purchase enough.

Shape 'N Press (Lace Shaping Board)

I used fabric boards (covered cardboard) until the June Taylor's Shape 'N Press board became available. It is truly wonderful. This board measures 24" by 18" and has permanent lace shaping templates drawn right on the board. I never have to hunt for another lace shaping template again. Here is how I use it. I place my skirt, collar, pillow top or other project on top of the board with the desired template positioned correctly (I can see the template through the fabric), shape the lace along the template lines pinning into the board, spray starch lightly, re-pin the lace just to the fabric. Now I can move the fabric, correctly positioning the template, and start the process again. Did you notice, I never mentioned tracing the design on the fabric? With the Shape 'N Press, drawing on the fabric can be omitted so you never have to worry about removing fabric marker lines. I also use the flip side of the board. It has a blocking guide for bishops and round collars (sizes newborn to adult).

Shape 'N Press Board

Shish Kabob Sticks

I first learned about using wooden shish kabob sticks from some of the technical school sewing teachers in Australia. By the way, where does one get these wooden shish kabob sticks? At the grocery store! If you can only find the long ones, just break them in half to measure 5" or 6" long and use the end with the point to push and to hold laces (or other items) as they go into the sewing machine. These sticks are used instead of the usual long pin or worse still, seam ripper that I have used so often. Using this stick is a safety technique as well as an efficient technique.

Making A Lace Shaping Board or Fabric Board

If a lace shaping board is not available, a fabric board can be made from cardboard (cake boards, pizza boards or a cut up box) covered with fabric or paper. A child's bulletin board or a fabric covered ceiling tile will work. Just staple or pin fabric or white typing paper or butcher paper over the board before you begin lace shaping. Just remember you must be able to pin into the board, use a bit of stray starch and iron on it.

Shaping Lace Diamonds

Lace diamonds can be used almost anywhere on heirloom garments. They are especially pretty at the point of a collar, on the skirt of a dress, at angles on the bodice of a garment, or all the way around a collar. The easiest way to make lace diamonds is to work on a fabric board with a diamond guide. You can make your diamonds as large or as small as you desire. I think you are really going to love this easy method of making diamonds with the fold back miter. Now, you don't have to remove those diamonds from the board to have perfect diamonds every time.

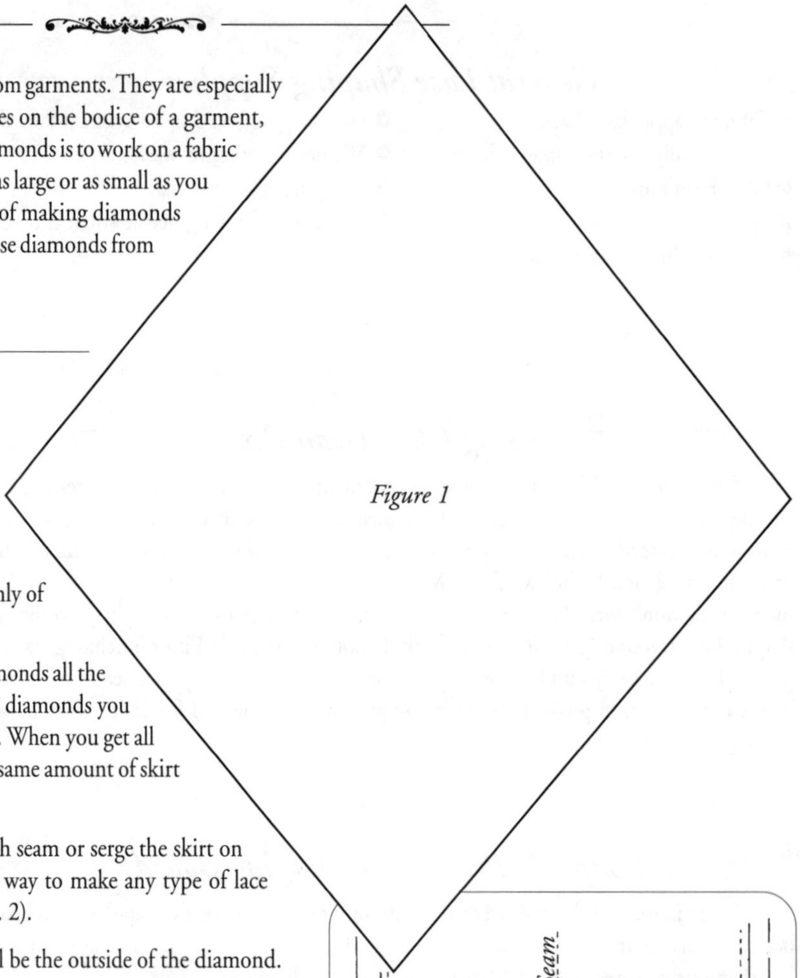

Making Lace Diamonds

Materials Needed
- ❁ Spray starch, iron, pins, fabric board
- ❁ Lace insertion
- ❁ Diamond guide

1. Draw the diamond guide or template (fig. 1).

2. Tear both skirt pieces. French seam or serge one side only of the skirt.

3. Working from the center seam you just made, draw diamonds all the way around the skirt. This way you can make any sized diamonds you want without worrying if they will fit the skirt perfectly. When you get all the way around both sides of the skirt you will have the same amount of skirt left over on both sides.

4. Simply trim the excess skirt away. Later you will French seam or serge the skirt on the other side to complete your skirt. This is the easy way to make any type of lace shaping on any skirt and it will always fit perfectly (fig. 2).

5. The guide or template, which you have just drawn, will be the outside of the diamond. Draw lines going into the diamond, bisecting each angle where the lace will be mitered. This is very important, since one of your critical pins will be placed exactly on this line. These bisecting lines need to be drawn about 2 inches long coming in from the angles of the diamonds (fig. 3). If you are making a diamond skirt, it is easier to draw your diamond larger and make your diamond shaping on the inside of the diamond. That way, the outside points of your diamond can touch when you are drawing all of your diamonds on the skirt.

6. As I said earlier, you can shape the laces for diamonds on either the outside or the inside of the template. I actually think it is easier to shape your laces on the inside of the template.

7. Place your skirt with the drawn diamonds on a fabric board.

8. Place the lace flat and guiding it along the inside of the drawn template, put a pin at point A and one at point B where the bisecting line goes to the inside (fig. 4a). The pin goes through both the lace and the fabric into the fabric board.

9. Guiding the edge of the lace along the drawn template line, place another pin into the fabric board through the lace (and the fabric skirt) at point C and another one at point D on the bisecting line (fig. 4b).

10. Fold back the lace right on top of itself. Remove the pin from the fabric board at point D, replacing it this time to go through both layers of lace rather than just one. Of course, the pin will not only go through both layers of lace but also through the skirt and into fabric board (fig. 5).

Figure 1

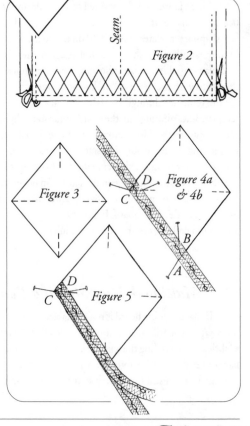

Figure 2

Figure 3

Figure 4a & 4b

Figure 5

11. Take the lace piece and bring it around to once again follow the outside line. You magically have a folded miter already in place (see fig. 6).

12. Guiding further, with the edge of the lace along the inside of the drawn template line, place another pin into the fabric board through the lace at point E and another at point F on the bisecting line (fig. 6).

13. Fold the lace right back on top of itself. Remove the pin at point F, replacing it this time to go through both layers of lace rather than just one (fig. 7).

14. Take the lace piece and bring it around to once again follow the outside line. You magically have a folded miter already in place (fig. 8).

15. Guiding further, with the edge of the lace along the inside of the drawn template line, place another pin into the lace at point G and another pin at point H on the bisecting line.

16. Fold the lace right back on top of itself. Remove the pin at point H, replace it this time to go through both layers of lace rather than just one.

17. Take the lace piece and bring it around to once again follow the outside line. You magically have a folded miter already in place (fig. 9).

18. At the bottom of the lace diamond, let the laces cross at the bottom. Remove the pin at point B and replace it into the fabric board through both pieces of lace. Remove the pin completely at point A (fig. 10).

19. Taking the top piece of lace, and leaving in the pin at point B only, fold the lace under and back so that it lies on top of the other piece of lace. You now have a folded in miter for the bottom of the lace.

20. Put a pin in, now, at point B (fig. 11). Of course you are going to have to cut away this long tail of lace. I think the best time to do that is before you begin your final stitching to attach the diamonds to the garment. It is perfectly alright to leave those tails of lace until your final stitching is done and then trim them.

21. You are now ready to spray starch and press the whole diamond shape. After spray starching and pressing the diamonds to the skirt, remove the pins from the fabric board and flat pin the lace shape to the skirt bottom. You are now ready to zigzag the diamond or machine entredeux stitch the diamond to the garment. Suggested zigzag settings are Width=2 to 3, Length=1 to 1¹/₂.

Finishing The Bottom Of The Skirt

These techniques are for finishing the bottom of a Diamond Skirt, a Heart Skirt, a Bow Skirt, or any other lace shaped skirt where the figures travel all the way around the bottom touching each other.

Method One

Using Plain Zigzag To Attach Diamonds (Or Other Shapes) To The Skirt

1. First, zigzag across the top of the diamond pattern, stitching from point A to point B, again to point A and finish the entire skirt (fig. 12). Your lace is now attached to the skirt all the way across the skirt on the top. If your fabric and diamonds have been spray starched well, you don't have to use a stabilizer when zigzagging these lace shapes to the fabric. The stitch width will be wide enough to cover the heading of the lace and go off onto the fabric on the other side. The length will be from ¹/₂" to 1", depending on the look that you prefer.

2. Zigzag all of the diamonds on the skirt, on the inside of the diamonds only (fig. 13).

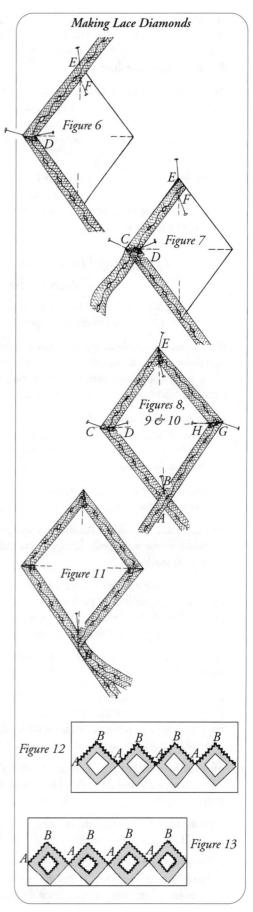

Making Lace Diamonds

Figure 6

Figure 7

Figures 8, 9 & 10

Figure 11

Figure 12

Figure 13

3. You are now ready to trim away the fabric of the skirt from behind the diamonds. Trim the fabric carefully from behind the lace shapes. The rest of the skirt fabric will now fall away leaving a diamond shaped bottom of the skirt (fig. 14). The lace will also be seen through the top of the diamonds.

4. If you are going to just gather lace and attach it at this point, then gather the lace and zigzag it to the bottom of the lace shapes, being careful to put extra fullness in the points of the diamonds (fig. 15). If your lace isn't wide enough to be pretty, then zigzag a couple of pieces of insertion or edging to your edging to make it wider (fig. 16).

5. If you are going to put entredeux on the bottom of the shapes before attaching gathered lace to finish it, follow the instructions for attaching entredeux to the bottom of a scalloped skirt given earlier in this lace shaping section. Work with short pieces of entredeux stitching from the inside points of the diamonds to the lower points of the diamonds on the skirt.

Finishing The Bottom Of The Skirt
Method Two
Using A Wing Needle Machine Entredeux Stitch To Attach Diamonds
(Or Other Lace Shapes) To The Skirt

1. If you are going to use the wing needle/entredeux stitch on your sewing machine to attach your diamonds or other lace shapes to the skirt, use the entredeux stitch for attaching all of the lace shapes to the skirt. Remember you must use a stabilizer when using the entredeux stitch/wing needle on any machine.

2. Place your stabilizer underneath the skirt, behind the shapes to be stitched. You can use small pieces of stabilizer which are placed underneath only a few shapes rather than having to have a long piece of stabilizer. Just be sure that you have stabilizer underneath these lace shapes before you begin your entredeux/wing needle stitching.

3. First, stitch the top side of the diamonds entredeux stitching from point A to point B all the way around the skirt. (fig. 17).

4. Secondly, stitch the inside of the diamonds using the entredeux stitch (fig. 18). Do not cut any fabric away at this point. Remember to continue using stabilizer for all entredeux/wing needle stitching.

5. You are now ready to gather your lace edging and machine entredeux it to the bottom of the skirt, joining the bottom portions of the diamonds at the same time you attach the gathered lace edging. If your machine has an edge joining or edge stitching foot with a center blade for guiding, this is a great place for using it.

6. Gather only a few inches of lace edging at a time. Butt the gathered lace edging to the flat bottom sides of the diamonds.

7. Machine entredeux right between the gathered lace edging and the flat side of the diamond. Remember, you are stitching through your laces (which are butted together, not overlapped), the fabric of the skirt and the stabilizer (fig. 19). Put a little extra lace gathered fullness at the upper and lower points of the diamonds.

8. After you have stitched your machine entredeux all the way around the bottom of the skirt, you have attached the gathered lace edging to the bottom of the skirt with your entredeux stitch.

9. Trim the fabric from behind the lace diamonds. Trim the fabric from underneath the gathered lace edging on the bottom of the skirt (fig. 20).

10. Either zigzag your folded miters in the angles of the diamonds or simply leave them folded in. I prefer to zigzag them (fig. 21). You also have the choice of cutting away the little folded back portions of the miters or leaving them for strength.

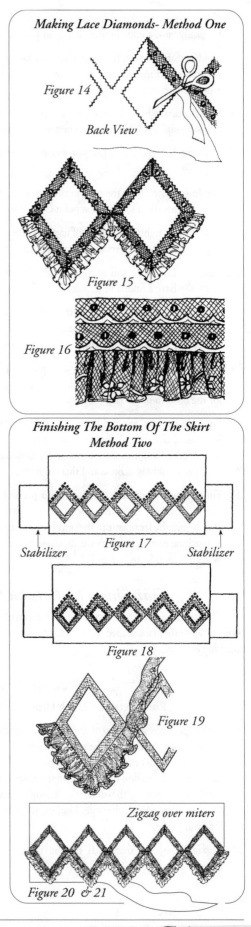

Making Lace Diamonds- Method One

Figure 14

Back View

Figure 15

Figure 16

Finishing The Bottom Of The Skirt
Method Two

Stabilizer   *Figure 17*   *Stabilizer*

Figure 18

Figure 19

Zigzag over miters

Figure 20 & 21

Shaping Flip-Flopped Lace Bows

Figure 1

I make lace bows using a technique called "flip-flopping" lace — a relatively unsophisticated name for such a lovely trim. I first saw this technique on an antique teddy I bought at a local antique store. It had the most elegant flip-flopped lace bow. Upon careful examination, I noticed the lace was simply folded over at the corners, then continued down forming the outline of the bow. The corners were somewhat square. Certainly it was easier than mitering or pulling a thread and curving. I found it not only looked easier, it was easier.

Follow the instructions for making a flip-flopped bow, using a bow template. This technique works just as well for lace angles up and down on a skirt. You can flip-flop any angle that traditionally would be mitered. It can be used to go around a square collar, around diamonds, and around any shape with an angle rather than a curve.

Flip-Flopping Lace

1. Trace the template onto the fabric exactly where you want to place bows (fig. 1). Remember, the easy way to put bows around a skirt is to fold the fabric to make equal divisions of the skirt. If you want a bow skirt which has bows all the way around, follow the directions for starting at the side to make the bows in the directions given for a diamond skirt.

2. Draw your bows on your garment or on a skirt where you want this lace shape.

3. Place your garment on your fabric board before you begin making your bow shapes. Beginning above the inside of one bow (above E), place the lace along the angle. The template is the inside guide line of the bow (fig. 2).

4. At the first angle (B), simply fold the lace so that it will follow along the next line (B-C) (fig. 3). This is called flip-flopping the lace.

5. Place pins sticking through the lace, the fabric, and into the shaping board. I like to place pins on both the inside edges and the outside edges. Remember to place your pins so that they lie as flat as possible.

6. The lines go as follows: A-B, B-C, C-D, D-A, E-F, F-G, G-H, H-E. Tuck your lace end under E, which is also where the first raw edge will end (fig. 4).

7. Cut a short bow tab of lace that is long enough to go around the whole tie area of the bow (fig. 4). This will be the bow tie!

8. Tuck in this lace tab to make the center of the bow (fig. 5). Another way to attach this bow tie is to simply fold down a tab at the top and the bottom and place it right on top of the center of the bow. That is actually easier than tucking it under. Since you are going to zigzag all the way around the bow "tie" it really won't matter whether it is tucked in or not.

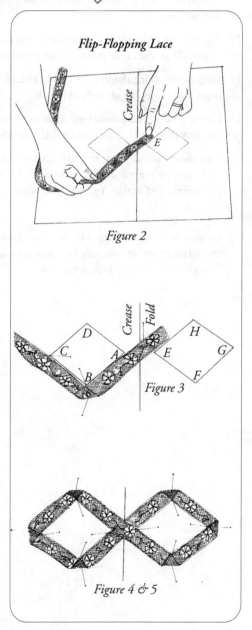

Flip-Flopping Lace

Figure 2

Figure 3

Figure 4 & 5

9. Spray starch and press the bow, that is shaped with the pins still in the board, with its bow tie in place (fig. 6). Remove pins from the board and pin the bow flat to the skirt or other garment. You are now ready to attach the shaped bow to the garment.

10. This illustration gives you ideas for making a bow two ways. First, the "A" side of the bow has just the garment fabric peeking through the center of the bow. Second, the "B" side of the bow illustrates what the bow will look like if you put a pintucked strip in the center. Both are beautiful (fig. 7).

11. If you prefer the bow to look like side (A), which has the fabric of the garment showing through the middle of the bow, follow these steps for completing the bow. Zigzag totally around the outside of the bow. Then, zigzag around the inside portions of both sides of the bow. Finally, zigzag around the finished bow "tie" portion (fig. 8). The bows will be attached to the dress.

12. If you prefer the bow to look like side (B), which will have pintucks (or anything else you choose) inside, follow the directions in this section. (These directions are when you have bows on areas other than the bottom of a skirt or sleeve or collar. If you have bows at the bottom of anything, then you have to follow the skirt directions given in the diamond skirt section.)

13. Zigzag the outside only of the bows all the way around. Notice that your bow "tie" will be partially stitched since part of it is on the outside edges.

14. I suggest pintucking a larger piece of fabric and cutting small sections which are somewhat larger than the insides of the bows (fig. 9).

15. Cut away fabric from behind both center sections of the bow. I lovingly tell my students that now they can place their whole fists inside the holes in the centers of this bow.

16. Place the pintucked section behind the center of the lace bows. Zigzag around the inside of the bows, which will now attach the pintucked section. From the back, trim away the excess pintucked section. You now have pintucks in the center of each side of the bow (fig. 10).

17. Go back and stitch the sides of the bow "tie" down. After you have zigzagged all the way around your bow "tie," you can trim away excess laces which crossed underneath the tie. This gives the bow tie a little neater look.

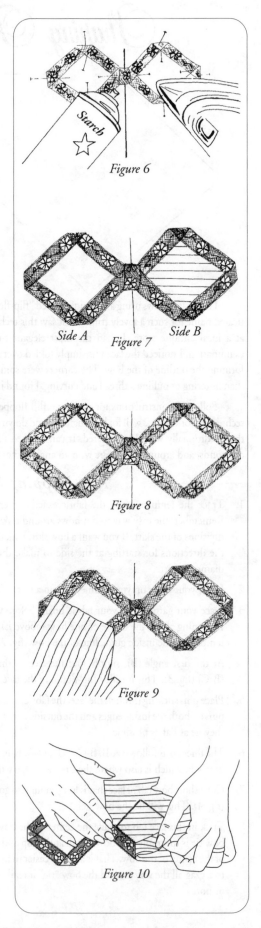

Figure 6

Side A   Figure 7   Side B

Figure 8

Figure 9

Figure 10

Tied Lace Bows

This method of bow shaping I saw for the first time years ago in Australia. It is beautiful and each bow will be a little different which makes it a very interesting variation of the flip-flopped bow. Your options on shaping the bow part of this cute bow are as follows:

1. You can flip-flop the bow
2. You can curve the bow and pull a string to make it round
3. You can flip-flop one side and curve the other side. Bows can be made of lace insertion, lace edging, or lace beading. If you make your tied lace bow of lace edging, be sure to put the scalloped side of the lace edging for the outside of the bow and leave the string to pull on the inside.

Materials Needed

✿ 1 yard to 1¼ yards lace insertion, edging or beading for one bow

Directions

1. Tie the lace into a bow, leaving equal streamers on either side of the bow (fig. 1).

2. Using a lace board, shape the bow onto the garment, using either the flip-flopped method or the pulled thread curved method.

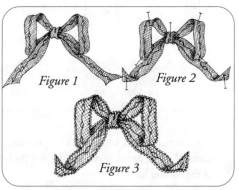

Figure 1   Figure 2

Figure 3

3. Shape the streamers of the bow using either the flip–flopped method or the pulled thread method (fig. 2).

4. Shape the ends of the streamer into an angle (fig. 2).

5. Zigzag or machine entredeux stitch the shaped bow and streamers to the garment (fig. 3).

Hearts-Fold Back Miter Method

Curving Lace

Since many heirloom sewers are also incurable romantics, it's no wonder hearts are a popular lace shape. Hearts are the ultimate design for a wedding dress, wedding attendants' clothing, or on a ring bearer's pillow. As with the other lace shaping discussed in this chapter, begin with a template when making hearts. When using our heart template, we like to shape our laces inside the heart design. Of course, shaping along the outside of the heart design is permitted also, so do whatever is easiest for you.

With the writing of the *Antique Clothing* book, I thought I had really figured out the easy way to make lace hearts. After four years of teaching heart making, I have totally changed my method of making hearts. This new method is so very easy that I just couldn't wait to tell you about it. After shaping your hearts, you don't even have to remove them from the skirt to finish the heart. What a relief and an improvement! Enjoy the new method of making hearts with the new fold back miters. It is so easy and you are going to have so much fun!

1. Draw a template in the shape of a heart. Make this as large or as small as you want. If you want equal hearts around the bottom of a skirt, fold the skirt into equal sections, and design the heart template to fit into one section of the skirt when using your chosen width of lace insertion.

2. Draw on your hearts all the way around the skirt if you are using several hearts. As always, when shaping lace, draw the hearts onto the fabric where you will be stitching the laces.

3. Draw a 2" bisecting line at the top into the center and at the bottom of the heart into the center (fig. 1).

NOTE: I would like to refresh your memory on lace shaping along the bottom of a skirt at this time. You make your hearts (or whatever else you wish to make) above the skirt while the skirt still has a straight bottom. Later after stitching your hearts (or whatever else) to the skirt, you cut away to make the shaped skirt bottom.

4. Lay the fabric with the hearts drawn on top, on top of the fabric board. As always, pin the lace shaping through the lace, the fabric and into the fabric board.

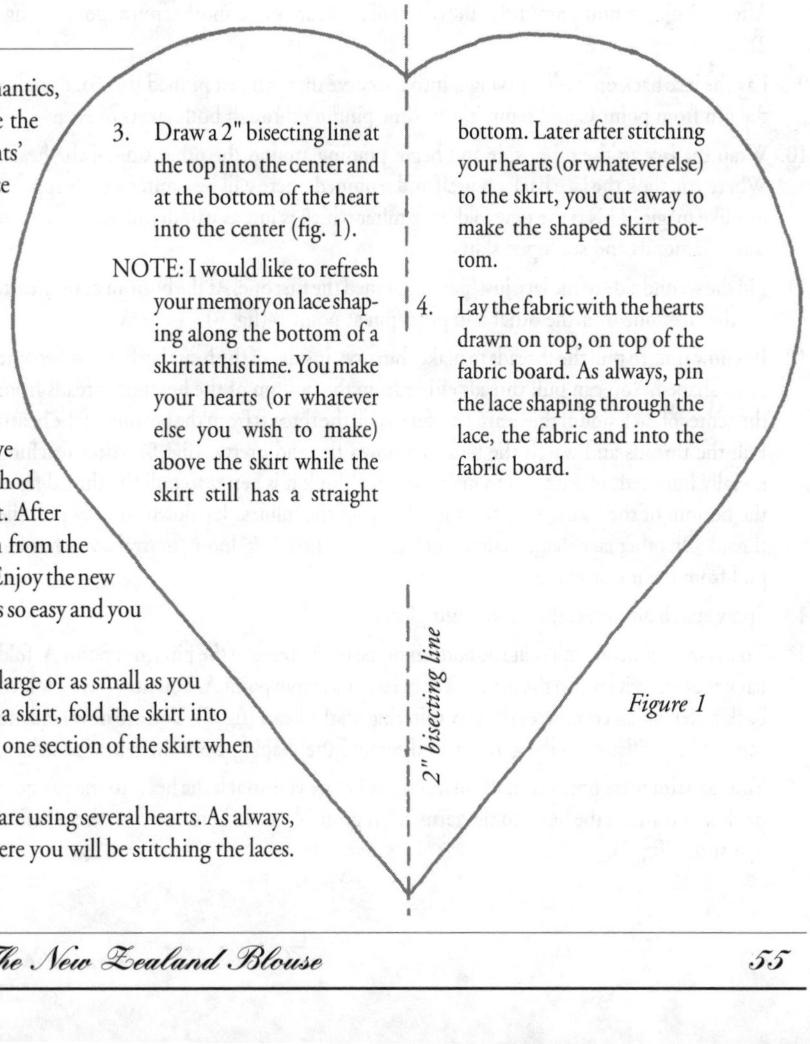

2" bisecting line

Figure 1

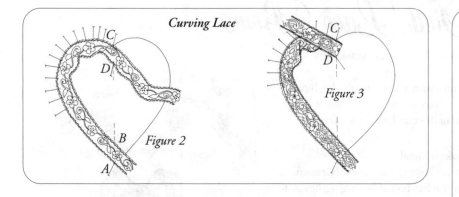

Figure 2

Figure 3

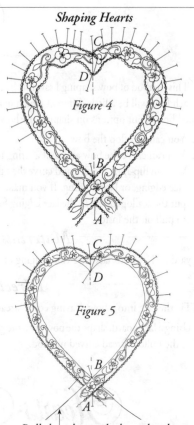

Shaping Hearts

Figure 4

Figure 5

Pull thread to make heart lay down

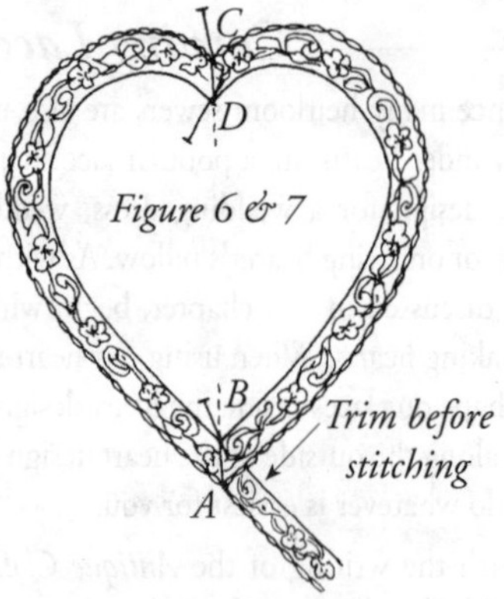

Figure 6 & 7

Trim before stitching

5. Cut one piece of lace which will be large enough to go all the way around one heart with about 4" extra. Before you begin shaping the lace, leave about 2" of lace on the outside of the bottom line.

6. Place a pin at point A. Beginning at the bottom of the heart, pin the lace on the inside of the heart template. The pins will actually be on the outside of the lace insertion; however, you are shaping your laces on the inside of your drawn heart template.

7. Work around the heart to point C, placing pins at $^1/_2$" intervals. Notice that the outside will be pinned rather tightly and the inside will be curvy. Note: One of our students who was a math teacher told me years ago while I was teaching this lace shaping, a very important fact. She said, "Martha did you know that a curved line is just a bunch of straight lines placed in a funny way?" She said this as I was trying to explain that it was pretty easy to get the straight lace pinned into a curve. Since I remembered as little about my math classes as possible, I am sure that I didn't know this fact. It makes it a lot easier to explain taking that straight lace and making a curve out of it to know that fact.

8. After finishing pinning around to the center of the heart, place another pin at point D (fig. 2).

9. Lay the lace back on itself, curving it into the curve that you just pinned (fig. 3). Remove the pin from point C and repin it, this time pinning through both layers of lace.

10. Wrap the lace to the other side and begin pinning around the other side of the heart. Where you took the lace back on itself and repinned, there will be a miter which appears just like magic. This is the new fold back miter which is just as wonderful on hearts as it is on diamonds and scalloped skirts.

11. Pin the second side of the lace just like you pinned the first one. At the bottom of the heart, lay the laces one over the other and put a pin at point B (fig. 4).

12. It is now time to pull the threads to make the curvy insides of the heart lay flat and become heart shaped. You can pull threads either from the bottom of the heart or threads from the center of each side of the heart. I prefer to pull the threads from the bottom of the heart. Pull the threads and watch the heart lay down flat and pretty. (fig. 5). After teaching literally hundreds of students to make hearts, I think it is better to pull the thread from the bottom of the heart. You don't need to help the fullness lay down; simply pull the thread. On other lace shaped curves such as a scalloped skirt, loops, or ovals, you have to pull from the inside curve.

13. Spray starch and press the curves into place.

14. To make your magic miter at the bottom of the heart, remove the pin from point A, fold back the lace so it lays on the other piece of lace, and repin point A. You now have a folded back miter which completes the easy mitering on the heart (fig. 6). You are now ready to pin the hearts flat onto the garment and remove the shaping from the fabric board.

15. You can trim these bottom "tails" of lace away before you attach the heart to the garment or after you attach the heart to the garment. It probably looks better to trim them before you stitch (fig. 7).

16. You can attach the hearts just to the fabric or you can choose to put something else such as pintucks inside the hearts. If you have hearts which touch going all the way around a skirt, then follow the directions for zigzagging which are in the diamond section.

17. If you have one heart on a collar or bodice of a dress, then zigzag the outside first. If you choose to put something on the inside of each heart, cut away the fabric from behind the shape after zigzagging it to the garment. Then, put whatever you want to insert in the heart behind the heart shape and zigzag around the center or inside of

the heart. Refer to the directions on inserting pintucks or something else in the center of a lace shape in the flip-flopped bow section.

18. You can certainly use the entredeux/wing needle stitching for a beautiful look for attaching the hearts. Follow the directions for machine entredeux on the lace shaped skirt found in the diamond section of this lace shaping chapter.

19. After you cut away the fabric from behind the hearts, go back and zigzag over each mitered point (fig. 8). You then have the choice of either leaving the folded over section or of cutting it away. Personally, I usually leave the section because of the strength it adds to the miters. The choice is yours.

Figure 8

Scalloped Skirt

I have always loved scalloped skirts. The first one that I ever saw intimidated me so much that I didn't even try to make one for several years after that. The methods which I am presenting to you in this section are so easy that I think you won't be afraid to try making one of my favorite garments. Scalloping lace can be a very simple way to finish the bottom of a smocked dress or can be a very elaborate way to put row after row of lace scallops with curved pintucks in between those scallops. Plain or very elaborate - this is one of my favorite things in French sewing by machine. Enjoy!

Preparing The Skirt For Lace Scallops

Before I give you the steps below, which is one great way to prepare scallops on a skirt, let me share with you that you can also follow the instructions found under the beginning lace techniques for scallops as well as diamonds, hearts, teardrops or circles. These instructions are so that you can use any size scallop that you want to for any width skirt. How do you do that? Stitch or serge up one side seam of your whole skirt before placing the scallops.

1. Pull a thread and cut or tear your skirt. I usually put 88 inches in my skirt, two 44-inch widths - one for the front and one for the back. Make the skirt length the proper one for your garment. Sew one side seam.

2. Trace one scallop on each side of the side seam. Continue tracing until you are almost at the edge of the fabric. Leave a seam allowance beyond the last scallops and trim away the excess (fig. 1).

3. Now you are ready to shape the lace along the template lines.

Pinning The Lace Insertion To The Skirt Portion On The Fabric Board

1. Cut enough lace insertion to go around all of the scallops on the skirt. Allow at least 16 inches more than you measured. You can later use the excess lace insertion in another area of the dress. If you do not have a piece of insertion this long, remember to piece your laces so that the pieced section will go into the miter at the top of the scallop.

2. Pin the lace insertion to the skirt (one scallop at a time only) by poking pins all the way into the fabric board, through the bottom lace heading and the fabric of the skirt. Notice on (figure 2) that the bottom of the lace is straight with the pins poked into the board. The top of the lace is rather "curvy" because it hasn't been shaped to lie flat yet.

3. As you take the lace into the top of the first scallop, carefully place a pin into the lace and the board at points C and D. Pinning the D point is very important. That is why you drew the line bisecting the top of each scallop (fig. 2). Pin the B point at exactly the place where the flat lace crosses the line you drew to bisect the scallop.

Preparing The Skirt For Lace Scallops

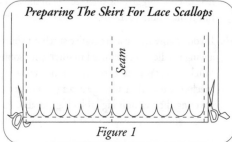

Figure 1

Pinning The Lace Insertion

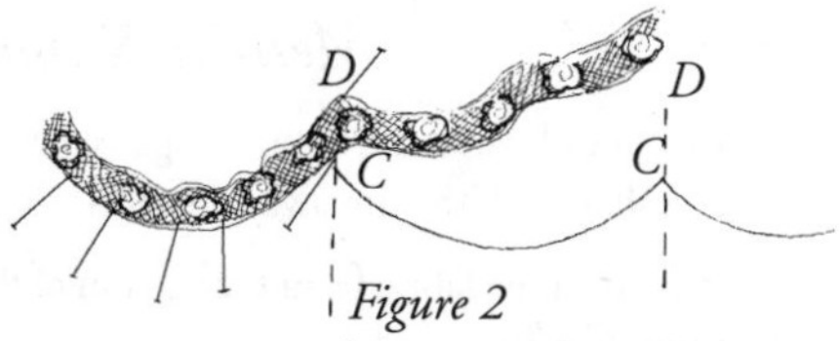

Figure 2

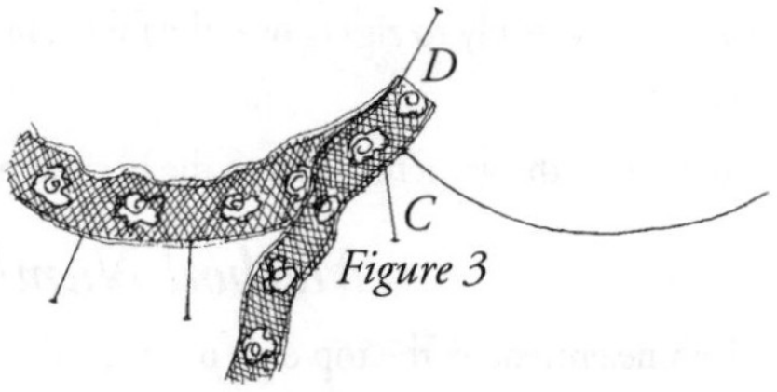

Figure 3

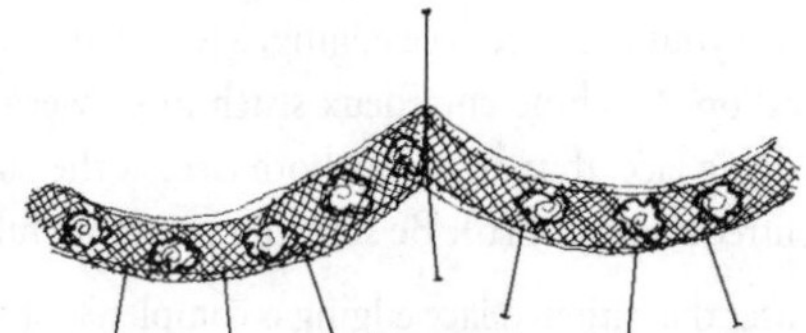

Figure 4

4. Fold back the whole piece of lace onto the other side (fig. 3). Remove the pin at C and repin it to go through both layers of lace. Leave the pin at point D just as it is.

5. Then fold over the lace to place the next section of the lace to travel into the next part of the scallop (fig.4).

NOTE: If a little bit of that folded point is exposed after you place the lace into the next scallop, just push it underneath the miter until the miter looks perfect (fig. 5). I call this "mushing" the miter into place.

6. To shape the excess fullness of the top of the scallop, simply pull a gathering thread at the center point of each scallop until the lace becomes flat and pretty (fig. 6).

7. Place a pin in the lace loop you just pulled until you spray starch and press the scallop flat. Remember, it is easier to pull the very top thread of the lace, the one which makes a prominent scallop on the top of the lace. If you break that thread, go in and pull another one. Many laces have as many as 4 or 5 total threads which you can pull. Don't worry about that little pulled thread; when you zigzag the lace to the skirt or entredeux stitch it to the skirt, simply trim away that little pulled thread. The heaviness of the zigzag or the entredeux stitch will secure the lace to the skirt.

8. Spray starch and press each scallop and miter after you finish shaping them.

9. After finishing with the section of scallops you have room for on that one board, pin the laces flat to the skirt and begin another section of your skirt (fig 7). You have the choice here of either zigzagging each section of the skirt as you complete it, or waiting until you finish the whole skirt.

10. If you choose to use a decorative stitch on your sewing machine (entredeux stitch with a wing needle) you will need to stitch with some sort of stabilizer underneath the skirt. Stitch 'n Tear is an excellent one. Some use tissue paper, others prefer wax paper or adding machine paper. Actually, the paper you buy at a medical supply store that doctors use for covering their examining tables is great also. As long as you are stitching using a wing needle and heavy decorative stitching, you really need a stabilizer.

11. If you have an entredeux stitch on your sewing machine, you can stitch entredeux at both the top and bottom of this scalloped skirt (fig. 8). There are two methods of doing this.

Method Number One

1. After you finish your entredeux/wing needle stitching on both the top and the bottom of the scalloped skirt, trim away the fabric from behind the lace scallop.

2. Carefully trim the fabric from the bottom of the skirt also, leaving just a "hair" of seam allowance (fig. 9).

3. You are now ready to zigzag over the folded in miters (fig. 10). Use a regular needle for this zigzag.

4. Now zigzag the gathered laces to the bottom of this machine created entredeux.

Method Number Two

1. Machine entredeux the top only of the scallop (fig. 11a). Don't cut anything away.

2. Butt your gathered lace edging, a few inches at a time, to the shaped bottom of the lace scallop. Machine entredeux stitch in between the flat scalloped lace and the gathered edging lace, thus attaching both laces at the same time you are stitching in the machine entredeux (fig. 11b). Be sure you put more fullness at the points of the scallop.

3. After the gathered lace edging is completely stitched to the bottom of the skirt with your machine entredeux, cut away the bottom of the skirt fabric as closely to the stitching as possible (fig. 12).

4. Zigzag over your folded in miters (fig. 12a).

5. If you are going to attach the lace to the fabric with just a plain zigzag stitch, you might try (Width=1$\frac{1}{2}$ to 2, Length=1 to 1$\frac{1}{2}$). You want the zigzag to be wide enough to completely go over the heading of the laces and short enough to be strong. If you are zigzagging the laces to the skirt, zigzag the top only of the lace scallops (see fig. 13).

6. After you zigzag the top only of this skirt, carefully trim away the bottom portion of the fabric skirt, trimming all the way up to the stitches (fig. 13).

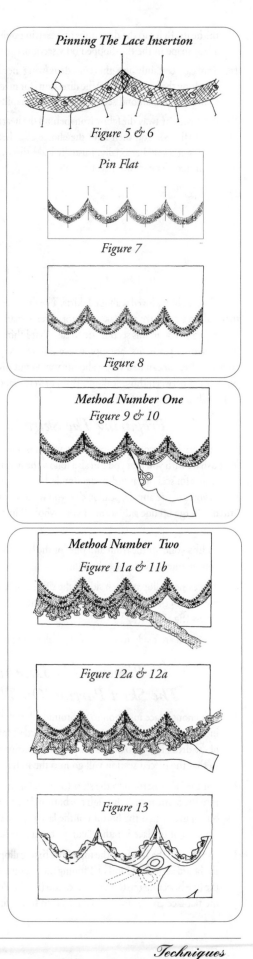

Pinning The Lace Insertion

Figure 5 & 6

Pin Flat

Figure 7

Figure 8

Method Number One
Figure 9 & 10

Method Number Two
Figure 11a & 11b

Figure 12a & 12a

Figure 13

7. Now you have a scalloped skirt. Later you might want to add entredeux to the bottom of the scalloped skirt. It is perfectly alright just to add gathered laces to this lace scallop without either entredeux or machine stitched entredeux. Just treat the bottom of this lace scallop as a finished edge; gather your lace edging and zigzag to the bottom of the lace (see fig. 14).

Finishing The Center Of The Miter
After Attaching It To The Skirt and Trimming Away The Fabric From Behind the Scallops

I always zigzag down the center of this folded miter. You can leave the folded lace portion in the miter to make the miter stronger or you can trim away the folded portion after you have zigzagged over the miter center (fig. 14).

Sewing Hand-Gathered French Lace To Entredeux Edge

1. Gather the lace by hand by pulling the thread in the heading of the lace. I use the scalloped outside thread of the heading first since I think it gathers better than the inside threads. Distribute gathers evenly.

2. Trim the side of the entredeux to which the gathered lace is to be attached. Side by side, right sides up, zigzag the gathered lace to the trimmed entredeux (Width=1$^1/_2$; Length=2) (fig. 15).

3. Using a wooden shish kabob stick, push the gathers evenly into the sewing machine as you zigzag. You can also use a pick or long pin of some sort to push the gathers evenly into the sewing machine.

HINT: To help distribute the gathers evenly fold the entredeux in half and half again. Mark these points with a fabric marker. Before the lace is gathered, fold it in half and half again. Mark the folds with a fabric marker. Now gather the lace and match the marks on the entredeux and the marks on the lace (fig. 16).

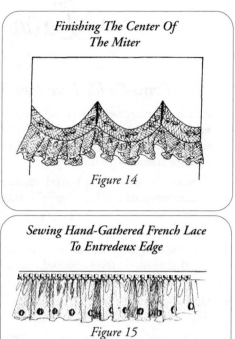

Finishing The Center Of The Miter

Figure 14

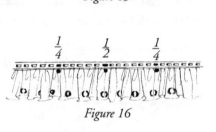

Sewing Hand-Gathered French Lace To Entredeux Edge

Figure 15

$\frac{1}{4}$ $\frac{1}{2}$ $\frac{1}{4}$

Figure 16

French Seam

1. Place the fabric pieces with wrong sides together.

2. Stitch a row of tiny zigzag stitches (L 1.0, W 1.0) $^3/_{16}$" outside the seam line (see fig. 1).

3. Press the seam flat and trim away the seam allowance outside the zigzags (fig. 1).

4. Open out the fabric and press the seam to one side.

5. Fold the fabric along the seam line with right sides together, encasing the zigzag stitching (fig. 2).

6. Stitch a $^3/_{16}$" seam, enclosing the zigzag stitching (fig. 3).

7. Press the seam to one side.

NOTE: A serged, rolled edge may be used for the first seam, when the fabric pieces are wrong sides together. No trimming will be needed, as the serger cuts off the excess seam allowance. If a pintuck foot is available, use it to stitch the second seam for either the zigzag or serger method. Place the tiny folded seam into a groove of the foot so that the needle will stitch right along beside the little roll of fabric (fig. 4).

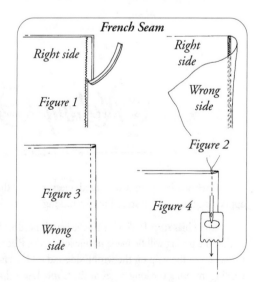

French Seam

Right side   *Right side*

Figure 1   *Wrong side*

Figure 2

Figure 3

Figure 4

Wrong side

Extra-Stable Lace Finishing

Extra-Stable Lace Finish for Fabric Edges

1. If the lace is being attached to a straight edge of fabric, pin the heading of the lace to the right side, $^1/_4$" or more from the cut edge, with the right side of the lace facing up and the outside edge of the lace extending over the edge of the fabric. Using a short straight stitch, stitch the heading to the fabric (fig. 1).

2. If the lace is being attached to a curved edge, shape the lace around the curve as you would for lace shaping; refer to "Lace Shaping" found on page 40. Pull up the threads in the lace heading if necessary. Continue pinning and stitching the lace as directed in Step 1 above (fig. 2).

3. Press the seam allowance away from the lace, toward the wrong side of the fabric (fig. 3). If the edge is curved or pointed, you may need to clip the seam allowance in order to press flat (fig. 4).

4. On the right side, use a short, narrow zigzag to stitch over the lace heading, catching the fold of the pressed seam allowance (fig. 5).

5. On the wrong side, trim the seam allowance close to the zigzag (fig. 6).

NOTE: Extra-Stable Lace Finish for Fabric Edges can be used for lace shaping (figs. 7 & 8).

Extra-Stable Lace Finish for Fabric Edges

Figure 7

Figure 8

Extra-Stable Lace Finishing

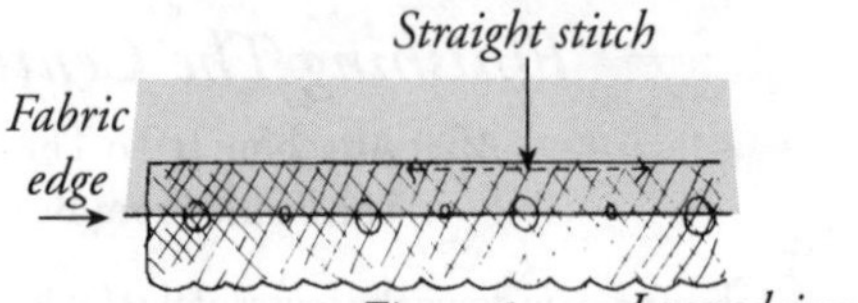

Figure 1

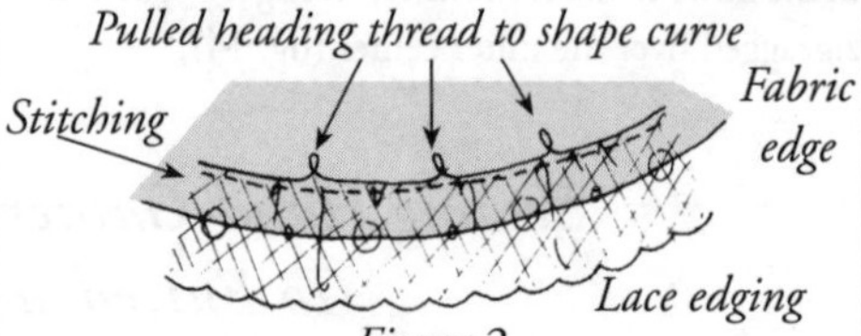

Figure 2

Figure 3

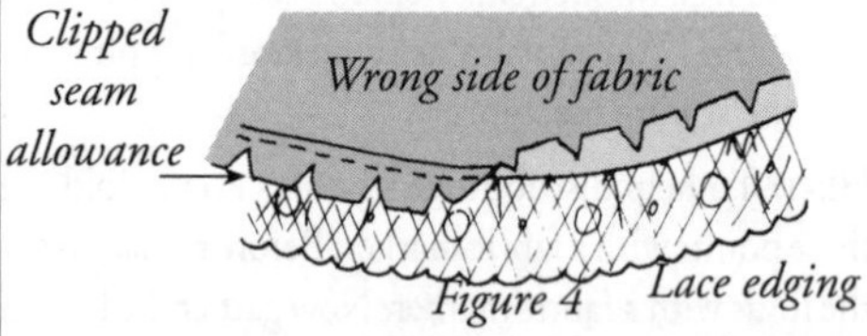

Figure 4

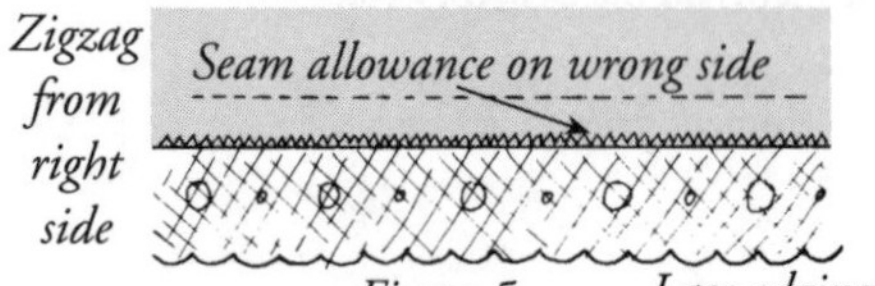

Figure 5

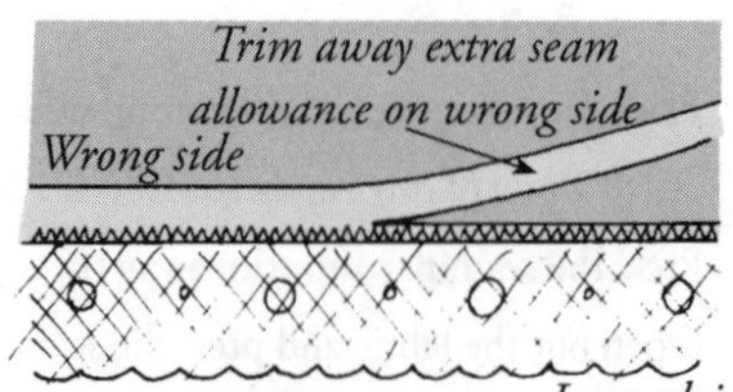

Figure 6

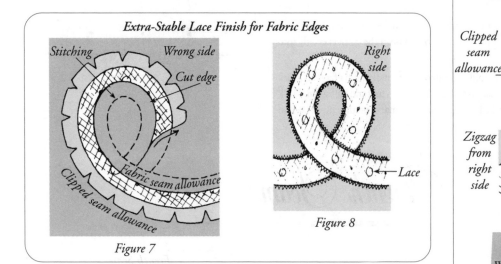

Making Piping

If self-made piping will be used, measure all of the places it will be applied and use these instructions for making it:

Cut a bias strip $1^1/_4$" wide by the length needed. Bias may be pieced so that the piping will be made in one long strip. Place tiny cording along the center of the strip on the wrong side and fold the fabric over the cording, meeting the long edges of the fabric. Use a zipper foot to stitch close to the cording (fig. A).

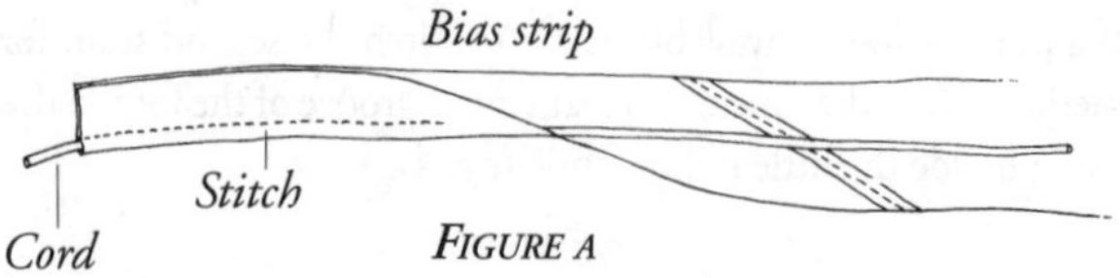

FIGURE A

Cutwork is a type of embroidery in which an area of fabric is cut away and the edges are bound with a satin stitch. Using the sewing machine to first reinforce an area to be cut away, trimming the fabric and then satin stitching the edge makes it quick and easy. Cutwork can be used on collars, cuffs, blouse fronts and skirt hems.

General Supplies

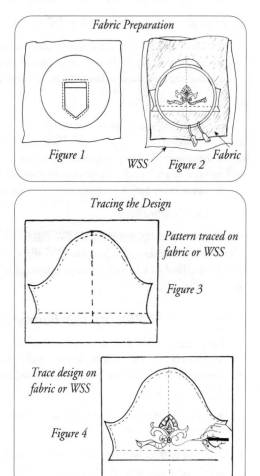

Fabric Preparation

Figure 1

WSS   *Figure 2*   Fabric

Tracing the Design

Pattern traced on fabric or WSS

Figure 3

Trace design on fabric or WSS

Figure 4

* Darning foot, open darning foot or darning spring
* Machine embroidery hoop (wooden or spring)
* Needles (#70 to #90)
* Light weight or machine embroidery thread
* Stabilizer (water soluble, tear away, or liquid)

* Water soluble pen or pencil
* Small, sharp pointed scissors
* Extra fine permanent marker
* White water soluble pen
* Bobbin case (optional)
* Open toe appliqué foot
* Interfacing
* Appliqué Scissors

Stabilizers

Water soluable stabilizer (WSS) is preferred since it can be washed away without putting stress on the stitches or bars when it is removed. It will not leave any residue or stiffness when removed completely. Use 2 to 4 layers, depending on body of base fabric and the heaviness and width of the stitches.

Fabric Used for Cutwork

The most often used fabric for cutwork is linen or linen-like fabrics. The fabric should not be too loosely woven and should have enough body to support the stitches. More than one layer of fabric can be used to add body. The fabric can be interfaced with a lightweight fusible interfacing prior to any stitching. If the fabric for a collar is interfaced, back it with another layer of fabric. The fabric should be pretreated before any marking or stitching is done due to shrinkage and to remove finish from the factory.

General Cutwork Directions

Fabric Preparation

1. To determine the size of fabric for the cutwork, consider the position of the cutwork. The fabric should extend beyond the cutwork design in all directions so that it may be placed in the hoop. For example, when doing cutwork on a pocket edge, even though the pocket pattern itself is small, you must start with a piece of fabric large enough to fit in a hoop (fig. 1). Another example would be when placing cutwork on the edge of a sleeve, the fabric must be large enough to contain the whole cutwork design plus enough fabric on the edges to be held in the hoop (fig. 2).

2. Press and starch the pretreated fabric to remove all of the wrinkles and give the fabric some body. Several applications of starch can be used.

3. Interface the fabric if needed.

Tracing the Design

There are two ways to trace the pattern piece and design onto the fabric:

1. See-through fabric: Place the pattern under the fabric. Trace the pattern onto the fabric using a water or air soluable pen (fig. 3). Use of a light box, if available, is helpful. Follow manufacturers' instructions for the marking pen or pencil. Sometimes heat from an iron may set these marks, so always test first!

2. Opaque fabric (cannot see through): When using a dark colored or opaque fabric the design must be traced onto a layer of WSS. The WSS is then placed on top of the fabric in the desired position (fig. 4). Use the Pigma pen when tracing a design to be placed on a light colored opaque fabric. Use the white washable marker to trace the design to be placed on top of a dark fabric.

3. Mark the cutting and seam lines.

4. Mark the center front or any other important marking lines.

5. DO NOT CUT OUT AT THIS TIME (fig. 5).

6. Mark all areas to be cut out with an "X" (fig. 6).

7. Richelieu bar placement can also be marked with a line extending beyond the area to be cut away (fig. 7). Richelieu bars connect both sides of an open area, helping to stabilize the area. Bars are not necessary for small cut away areas.

a. Straight Richeleiu Bars:

These bars should be no longer than about $1/2$ inch long. When the bar is too long, it will not stabilize the area adequately. These bars can be straight across, connecting one side of the opening to the opposite side (fig. 8) For an open area that has one side larger than another, as a half circle, the bars can be placed at angles to form an open "V" or "V's" (fig. 9). Use as many bars as necessary to stabilize the open area (fig. 10).

b. Divided Richelieu Bars:

A wider width open area may be too wide for a straight bar. In this case, a DIVIDED bar will be formed to look like a "Y" (fig. 11). For a large open area, the space must be stabilized with bars of any shape connected to each other AND the sides of the open area (fig. 12).

Placing the Fabric in a Hoop

1. For machine embroidery, the fabric is placed in the hoop opposite from hand embroidery. The right side of the fabric will be facing up, the wrong side is down toward the bed of the machine (fig. 13). Stabilizer should be added under the two layers.

2. When the pattern is traced onto the WSS, pin or baste the WSS in position on top of the fabric.

3. Place one to three layers of WSS to wrong side of the fabric.

4. When the design size is larger than the hoop, baste all layers together so that the pattern, the fabric and the WSS under the fabric will not shift when changing the hoop position (fig. 14).

Preparing the Sewing Machine for Cutwork

Thread and Tension

Thread machine with matching machine embroidery thread in top and bobbin. The tension is balanced at this time.

Cutwork with an Appliqué Foot

1. Place open toe appliqué foot on machine.

2. With a straight stitch, length of 1 to 1.5 mm, stitch around all areas to be cut away. Stitching over ALL of the lines in the design (not just areas to be cut away) will add a padding under the final satin stitch (fig. 15). This straight stitch will prevent stretching when the fabric is cut away from the design.

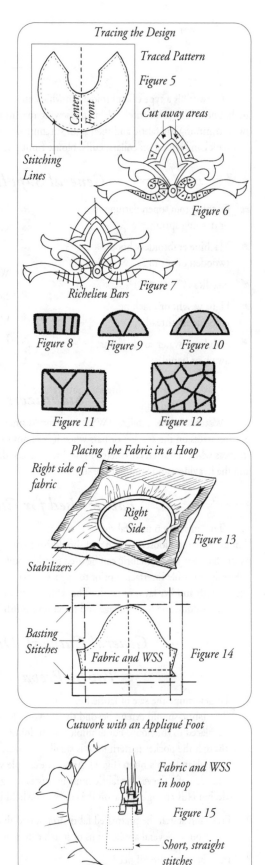

Tracing the Design

Traced Pattern

Figure 5

Center Front

Cut away areas

Stitching Lines

Figure 6

Figure 7

Richelieu Bars

Figure 8   Figure 9   Figure 10

Figure 11   Figure 12

Placing the Fabric in a Hoop

Right side of fabric

Right Side

Figure 13

Stabilizers

Basting Stitches

Fabric and WSS

Figure 14

Cutwork with an Appliqué Foot

Fabric and WSS in hoop

Figure 15

Short, straight stitches

3. Stitch over the straight stitch with a short narrow zig zag, width of 0.5 to 1 mm and length of 1 mm (fig. 16). This is not a satin stitch. Stitch all of the design lines that are in the hoop. You can move the hoop to complete all of the design lines before cutting any area away. The zigzag stitch will help prevent the fabric from pulling away from the stitches when the areas are cut away.

4. With the fabric still in the hoop, trim the fabric close to the stitching from the appropriate areas leaving the lower layer(s) of WSS in place (fig. 17). The lower, uncut layers of WSS will prevent distortion of the cut away areas. If the design is on the top layer of WSS, this will be cut away also. Use sharp, small pointed scissors to cut away, being careful not to cut the stitches. Appliqué scissors are very useful.

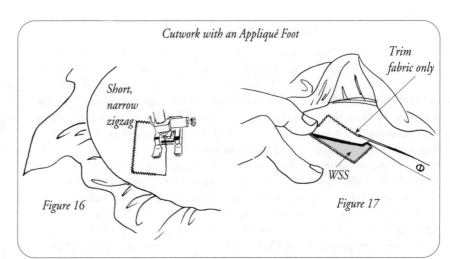

Cutwork with an Appliqué Foot

Short, narrow zigzag

Figure 16

Trim fabric only

WSS

Figure 17

5. LOOK AT THE DESIGN. The Richelieu bars and the satin stitches to cover the bars and raw edges are worked background to foreground. Place design back under the needle at the appropriate starting point.

6. Set up the sewing machine for a satin stitch: Loosen the top thread tension so that the bobbin thread will pull the top thread to the back for a smoother stitch on the right side. Set stitch length at satin stitch. The stitch width will be adjusted during the stitching.

7. Richelieu bars are completed before the final satin stitching is done.

Straight Richelieu Bars

1. Pull up bobbin thread near first bar, place both upper and lower threads under and behind the foot (fig. 18). Take three to six short straight stitches (satin stitch length) to TIE-ON (this is done each time you start a new area), ending at first bar placement (fig. 19). Cut thread ends close to the first stitch.

2. Lift foot and move fabric across the opening so that needle will pierce opposite side beyond the previous zigzag stitch (fig. 20). Lower foot and take one stitch. This is a "WALK" stitch over the opening. You have not actually "stitched" through the opening, but just moved the thread over it. You can see two separate threads, the top and the bobbin thread. Repeat at least two more times so that there will be three walked stitches over the opening (6 threads) (fig. 21). These walked stitches will form the base for the bars. More or fewer walk stitches can be taken to make a thicker or narrower finished bar.

3. Change the stitch width to cover the walked stitches (1 to 2 mm), usually a little narrower than the final satin stitching will be. This width will be determined by the number of walked stitches. Satin stitch over the walked stitches only within the opening (fig. 22) being certain all walk threads are caught in the satin stitch and covered completely.

4. Straight stitch on the fabric to the next bar within the same opening. Repeat as above. Finish all bars within this area (fig. 23).

You can finish all of the walk stitches within an area before satin stitching or finish each bar individually.

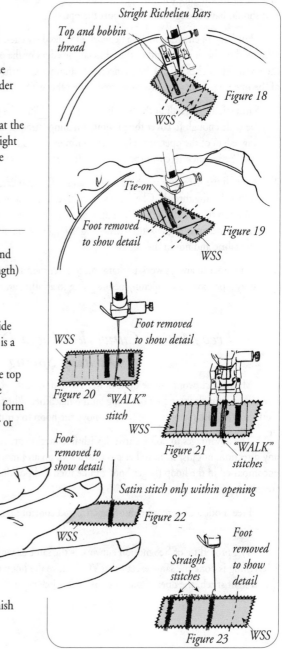

Straight Richelieu Bars

Top and bobbin thread

Figure 18

WSS

Tie-on

Foot removed to show detail

Figure 19

WSS

WSS

Foot removed to show detail

Figure 20

"WALK" stitch

WSS

Figure 21

"WALK" stitches

Foot removed to show detail

Satin stitch only within opening

Figure 22

WSS

Straight stitches

Foot removed to show detail

Figure 23

WSS

Divided Richelieu Bars

For a bar that is shaped like a "Y", begin at the upper left leg of the "Y". After tying on, move (WALK) from the tie-on stitch to the desired place on WSS within the opening (where the left and right legs of the "Y" join). Take a stitch IN the WSS (fig. 24). This will be the first SEGMENT of the bar. Walk to the top of the right leg of the "Y". Take a stitch into the fabric (fig. 25)(another segment). Walk back to the end of the first segment, take a stitch (fig. 26). You now have TWO walked stitches in this segment. Walk to the opposite side of the opening, creating the last segment of the "Y" bar (fig. 27). Take a stitch into the fabric just beyond the zigzag stitching. Walk to intersection in the WSS, take a stitch. Now two of the segments have two walked stitches (four threads). At this point, you can walk in any direction to increase the walk stitches in the segments and you can satin stitch one segment (if it has six threads) before ALL of the segments have six threads. You must finish the satin stitching at the fabric edge and not in the WSS (fig. 28). Sometimes it will be necessary to add an additional walked stitch so that the satin stitching will finish at the fabric edge and not in the WSS. The cut away area should have enough bars to support the opening.

For large open areas, make a network of walked stitches, connecting them to each other within the opening and to the fabric at the edges of the opening (fig. 29). All of these walked stitches MUST be connected to another segment or to the fabric at the edge of the opening. If they are not connected, when the WSS is rinsed away it will fall apart.

1. Satin stitch: After all of the bars are completed, adjust the stitch width so that it will be wide enough to cover the previous stitching (straight and zigzag stitch) AND the raw edges of the opening. The most commonly used is a stitch width of 2 mm or less. Satin stitch to cover the raw edges (fig. 30).

2. After all the necessary stitching is done and before moving to another area you must TIE-OFF the threads. Change stitch width to zero (satin stitch length), reposition fabric so that needle will go back into same hole it just came out of, and take three to six stitches next to the satin stitches (fig. 31). These tie off stitches should be done on the fabric and not in the cut away opening.

3. Remember to always work background to foreground. This may mean to satin stitch only a portion of an opening before going to another area (fig. 32).

Free Motion Cutwork using a Darning Foot or Darning Spring

Machine cutwork can be done in free motion, that is, with the feed dogs lowered or covered and the darning foot or spring on the machine. When doing free motion work, **YOU** are the stitch length. You have to move the hoop to create a stitch length.

The advantages to doing cutwork with free motion are the hoop can be moved in any direction, not just front to back as with a foot on and more of the design can be encompassed in the hoop (larger hoop can be used and position will not need to change as frequently).

Free motion does require more practice and control than does cutwork with the foot.

The procedure of free motion cutwork is the same as with the appliqué foot. Everything is done the same except that **YOU** move the hoop to create the stitch length of the straight stitch, the open zigzag and the satin stitch zigzag.

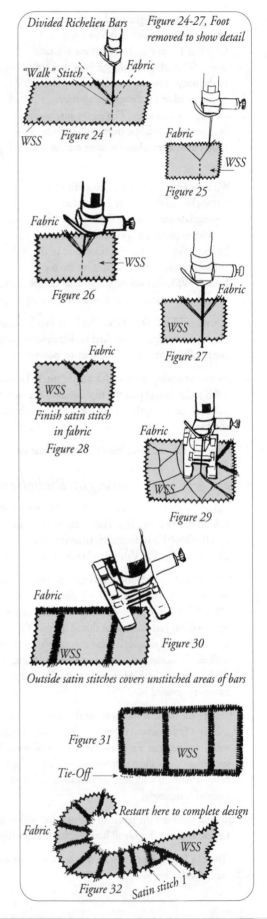

Divided Richelieu Bars

Figure 24-27, Foot removed to show detail

"Walk" Stitch

Fabric

WSS   *Figure 24*

Fabric

WSS

Figure 25

Fabric

WSS

Figure 26

Fabric

WSS

Figure 27

Fabric

WSS

Finish satin stitch in fabric

Figure 28

Fabric

WSS

Figure 29

Fabric

WSS

Figure 30

Outside satin stitches covers unstitched areas of bars

Figure 31

WSS

Tie-Off

Restart here to complete design

Fabric

WSS

Figure 32   Satin stitch 1"

Optional Cutwork Techniques

The following techniques can be done with the applique foot or free motion stitching.

Small Areas

Small areas can be cut away and then satin stitched without bars.

1. For a small area such as a tear drop, first straight stitch and then open zigzag.

2. Slit the fabric and the WSS in the opening down the middle with a "Y" at each end (fig. 33).

3. Satin stitch the opening, drawing in and encasing the raw edges as you stitch (fig. 34).

Larger Areas

Larger areas without bars can be treated in a similar manner.

1. First straight stitch and then open zigzag.

2. Slit the fabric and the WSS in the opening down the middle with a "Y" at each end (fig. 35).

3. Fold fabric and WSS to wrong side and glue with a glue stick to hold in place (fig. 36).

4. Satin stitch as described to encase the previous stitching and the folded edge.

5. Trim any excess fabric and WSS from the wrong side close to the satin stitch (fig. 37).

Larger Area with Bars

Larger areas with bars can be treated in a similar manner.

1. Straight stitch, open zigzag, and slit the fabric and the WSS as described above.

2. Fold fabric and WSS to wrong side and glue with a glue stick to hold in place (fig. 38).

3. Form the Richelieu bars as described previously.

4. Satin stitch to encase the previous stitching and the folded edge.

5. Trim any excess fabric and WSS from the wrong side close to the satin stitch.

Corded Edge Cutwork

A cord can be encased in the finishing satin stitch if desired. This will add strength to the open area.

1. Lay the cord next to the raw edge of the opening (fig. 39).

2. Encase the cord when doing the satin stitch.

Netting or Sheer Fabric for Support

A layer of netting or other sheer fabric can be placed behind the main fabric so that when an area is cut away, the netting or sheer fabric will support the opening. This will also eliminate the need for Richelieu bars in large cut away areas.

1. The netting or sheer fabric is placed to the wrong side of the base fabric before any stitching is done.

2. To facilitate cutting the base fabric away without cutting the netting or sheer fabric, place an extra layer of WSS **BETWEEN** the base fabric and the netting.

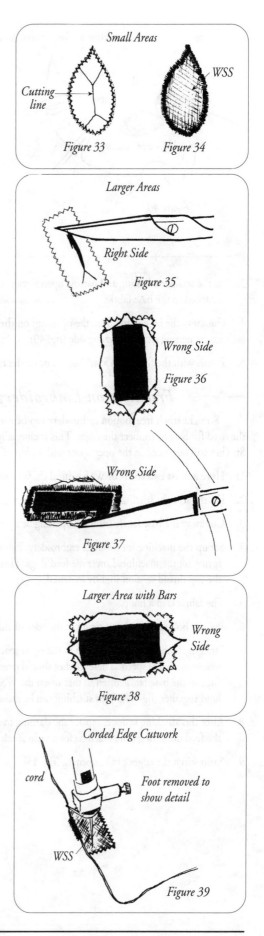

Small Areas

Cutting line

WSS

Figure 33

Figure 34

Larger Areas

Right Side

Figure 35

Wrong Side

Figure 36

Wrong Side

Figure 37

Larger Area with Bars

Wrong Side

Figure 38

Corded Edge Cutwork

cord

Foot removed to show detail

WSS

Figure 39

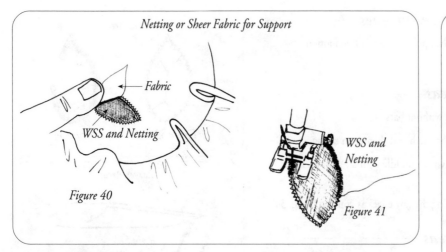

Fabric

WSS and Netting

Figure 40

WSS and Netting

Figure 41

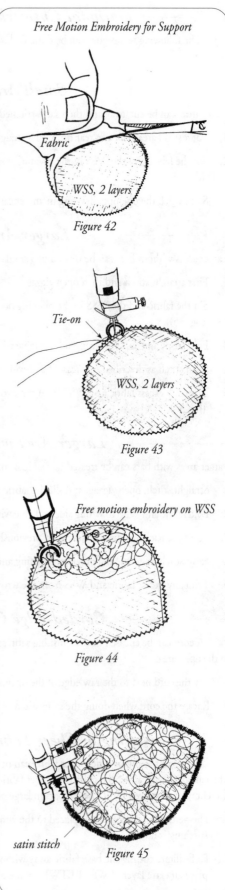

Fabric

WSS, 2 layers

Figure 42

Tie-on

WSS, 2 layers

Figure 43

Free motion embroidery on WSS

Figure 44

satin stitch

Figure 45

3. As the straight stitching and narrow open zigzag stitching are done the netting will be attached to the base fabric.

4. Cut away the base fabric from the openings on the right side of the fabric and the excess netting from the wrong side (fig. 40).

5. Finish with the final satin stitching to encase the raw edges (fig. 41).

Free Motion Embroidery for Support

Straight stitch free motion embroidery can be used to fill a cut away area eliminating the need for bars to connect the edges. This is especially helpful for large cut away areas. Stitches will be placed in the open space and on top of the WSS.

1. Have at least two layers of WSS behind the base fabric.

2. Do the straight stitching and the narrow open zigzag as described above.

3. Cut away the base fabric from the opening being careful to leave the WSS (fig. 42).

4. Set up the machine for machine embroidery. Place the open darning foot or darning spring on the machine. Lower the feed dogs. Thread tension should be balanced or the top thread tension slightly loosened.

5. The fabric is in a hoop.

6. Pull up bobbin thread and tie-on at the edge of the open area (fig. 43).

7. Straight stitch on top of the WSS in the open space by running the machine at a steady moderate speed. These stitches should overlap each other AND pierce the edge of the base fabric often so that when the WSS is washed away, the stitches will hold together (fig. 44). This stitching can be rather dense or more open and airy.

8. After this stitching is done, replace the darning foot with the appliqué foot and raise the feed dogs. Reset the machine for a satin stitch.

9. Satin stitch the edges of the opening (fig. 45).

Embroidery Techniques

Straight Stitch
(silk ribbon or floss)

Simply bring the needle up from under the fabric (fig. 1) and insert it down into the fabric a short distance in front of where the needle came up (fig. 2). It is an in and out stitch. Remember to pull the ribbon loosely for nice full stitches.

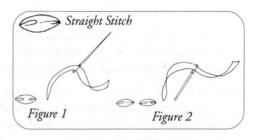

Straight Stitch

Figure 1 *Figure 2*

Japanese Ribbon Stitch
(silk ribbon)

Use any size ribbon. Bring the needle up from under the fabric, (fig. 1) loop it around and insert the needle down into the center of the ribbon a short distance in front of where the needle came up (fig. 2). Pull the ribbon so that the end curls in on itself loosely so that it does not disappear.

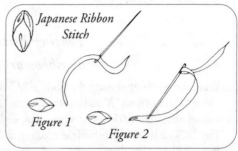

Japanese Ribbon Stitch

Figure 1 *Figure 2*

Stem/Outline Stitch
(silk ribbon or floss)

Worked from left to right, this stitch makes a line of slanting stitches. The thread is kept to the left and below the needle. Make small, even stitches. The needle is inserted just below the line to be followed, comes out to the left of the insertion point, and above the line, slightly.

1. Come up from behind at "a" and go down into the fabric again at "b" (see fig. 1). This is a little below the line. Come back up at "c" (fig. 1). This is a little above the line. Keep the thread below the needle.

2. Go back down into the fabric at "d" and come up a little above the line at "b" (fig. 2).

3. Continue working, always keeping the thread below the needle (fig. 3).

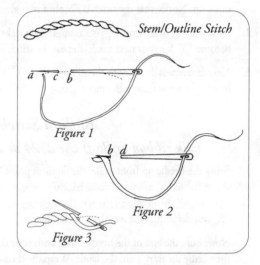

Stem/Outline Stitch

a c b

Figure 1

b d

Figure 2

Figure 3

French Knot
(silk ribbon or floss)

The most asked question about French knots is "How many wraps?". The number of wraps will depend on the size of the knot desired, the type of thread or floss being used, and personal preference. Generally, use one strand of floss or 2mm silk ribbon with one to two wraps per knot. If a larger knot is needed, use more strands of floss or larger silk ribbon. Often times, French knots will not lay flat on the fabric. To eliminate this problem, once the needle has been reinserted in the fabric (fig. 3), slip the wrapped floss or ribbon gently down the needle until it rests against the fabric. Hold the wraps against the fabric and slowly pull the floss or ribbon through the wraps to the wrong side. This will cause the knot to be formed on the surface of the fabric and not float above it.

1. Bring the needle up through the fabric (fig. 1).

2. Hold the needle horizontally with one hand and wrap the ribbon around the needle with the other hand (fig. 2). If you are using a single strand of floss, one or two wraps will create a small knot. If you are making French knots with 2mm silk ribbon, the knot will be larger. As stated above, the size of the knot varies with the number of strands of floss or the width of the silk ribbon being used.

3. While holding the tail of the ribbon to prevent it from unwinding off the needle, bring the needle up into a vertical position and insert it into the fabric just slightly beside where the needle came out of the fabric (fig. 3). Pull the ribbon or floss gently through the fabric while holding the tail with the other hand.

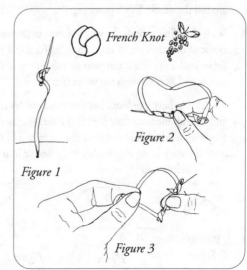

French Knot

Figure 2

Figure 1

Figure 3

Lazy Daisy Stitch
(silk ribbon or floss)

1. Bring the needle up through the center point if you are stitching a flower, and up just next to a vine or flower for leaves (fig. 1).

2. Insert the needle down into the same hole in which you came up. In the same stitch come through about $^1/_8$" to $^3/_8$" above that point (fig. 2). Wrap the ribbon behind the needle and pull the ribbon through, keeping the ribbon from twisting (fig. 3).

3. Insert the needle straight down into the same hole or very close to the same hole at the top of the loop (fig. 4). Notice in the side view of figure 4 that the needle goes down underneath the ribbon loop. The top view of figure 4 shows that the stitch is straight and will anchor the ribbon loop in place.

Feather Stitch
(silk ribbon or floss)

1. Bring the needle up through the fabric at "A" (fig. 1). Insert the needle down about $^1/_4$" to $^3/_8$" across from "A" and into the fabric at "B". In the same stitch bring the needle out of the fabric $^1/_4$" to $^3/_8$" down and slightly to the right of center at "C" (fig. 2). With the ribbon behind the needle, pull the ribbon through (fig. 3). This stitch is much like the lazy daisy only the needle does not insert into the same hole in which it came up. Notice that the stitch is simply a triangle.

2. Now you will begin working your triangle from right to left, or left to right. "C" will now become "A" for your next stitch. Repeat the stitch as in step 1 (fig. 4).

3. Next time repeat the stitch on the other side (fig. 5). The trick is that "A" and "B" will always be straight across from each other and that "A", "B", and "C" will line up vertically (fig. 6).

Bullion Stitch
(silk ribbon or floss) Use a 24 or 26 chenille needle.

1. Bring the needle up from under the fabric at point "A" and take a stitch down in "B" about $^3/_8$" to $^1/_4$" away and come back up through "A" beside (not through) the floss. Do not pull the needle all the way through (fig. 1). Note: The distance from "A" to "B" will determine the length of the bullion.

2. Now, hold the end of the needle down with your thumb. This will pop the point of the needle up away from the fabric. Wrap the floss or floss coming from point "A" around the needle 5 to 6 times (fig. 2).

3. With your finger, push the wraps of floss to the bottom of the needle next to the fabric so that they are all lined up tight (fig. 3). With your other hand, place your finger under the fabric and your thumb on top of the bullion and gently pull the needle and floss through the wraps (fig. 4).

4. You almost have a bullion, but first you most lay the coils over to the opposite side and take up the slack floss (fig. 5). To do this, lay the bullion over and place your finger under the fabric and your thumb on top of the bullion and gently pull the floss until the slack is out (fig. 6). Insert the needle into the fabric at the end of the bullion (fig. 7) and tie off.

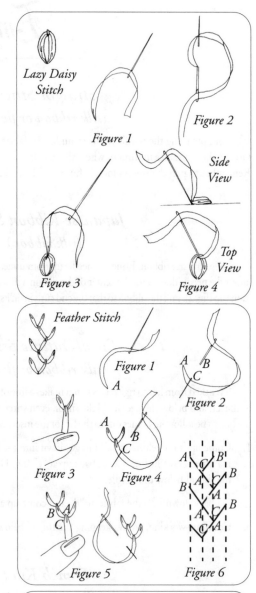

Lazy Daisy Stitch

Figure 1

Figure 2

Side View

Figure 3

Figure 4

Top View

Feather Stitch

Figure 1

Figure 2

Figure 3

Figure 4

Figure 5

Figure 6

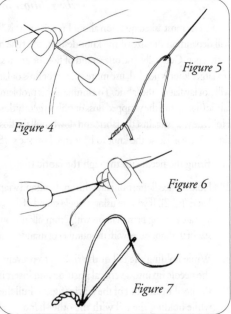

Figure 5

Figure 4

Figure 6

Figure 7

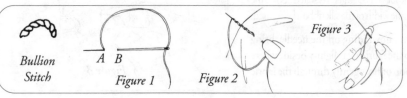

Bullion Stitch

A B

Figure 1

Figure 2

Figure 3

Chain Stitch
(silk ribbon or floss)

This is a glorified lazy daisy stitch that works beautifully on smocking and adds dimension to silk ribbon embroidery. It is a great outline stitch for stems and vines when done with one or two strands of floss.

1. Bring the needle up through the fabric at A. Swing the floss or ribbon around in a loop and hold the loop with your thumb (fig. 1).

2. While holding the loop, insert the needle in at B and out through C in one stitch. Keep the needle and floss or ribbon going over the loop (fig. 2).

3. Instead of inserting the needle to the other side like a lazy daisy, you will make another loop and insert the needle down, right beside C where you last came up, this will become a new A. In the same stitch, bring the needle through B and pull (fig. 3). Keep the needle over the loop.

4. Continue looping and stitching in an "A, B" - "A, B" sequence.

Fly Stitch
(silk ribbon or floss)

This stitch may be used for leaves at the base of flowers, it may be worked singly or in rows to give the appearance of ferns. This is an easy stitch to master and you will find many uses for it as fillers.

1. Come up at A. Insert the needle in the fabric at B, coming out of the fabric at C, making sure the loop of ribbon is below C (fig. 1). Keep the needle on top of the loop of ribbon.

2. The length of the anchor stitch is determined by the length of the stitch taken between C and D. The floss or ribbon comes out of the fabric at C and needle is inserted into the fabric at D. The longer the distance between D and D, the longer the anchor stitch. Gently pull the ribbon to the wrong side (fig. 2 & 3).

Side Stitch Rose
(silk ribbon)

This rose takes careful placement and looks particularly good in 4mm variegated ribbon. It is made up of side ribbon stitch petals; instead of piercing the ribbon in the middle, pierce on either the left or the right side of the ribbon, depending on which way you want the petal to turn.

1. Start with an upright stitch, piercing the ribbon on the right-hand side (fig. 1). This is petal 1. The petal will turn slightly to the right (fig. 2).

2. Place a second petal, slightly longer, to the right of petal 1, piercing on the left-hand side (fig. 3). This is petal 2.

3. Place a third petal, slightly shorter, to the left of petal 1, piercing the ribbon on the right-hand side. Place a fourth petal, the same length as the third, to the right of petal 2, piercing the ribbon on the left-hand side (fig. 4).

4. Place petals 5 and 6 at an angle on each side, piercing petal 5 on the right and petal 6 on the left (fig. 5).

5. Petals 7 and 8 drop below, leaving a small space below the top petals (fig. 6).

6. Work petals 9 and 10 from the base of petals 7 and 8 and over petals 1 and 2. The length of petals 9 and 10 will be 2/3 the length of petals 1 and 2. There will be a small gap in between petals 9 and 10 (fig. 7).

7. Petal 11 is placed between petals 9 and 10 and is slightly taller than petals 9 and 10 fig. 8).

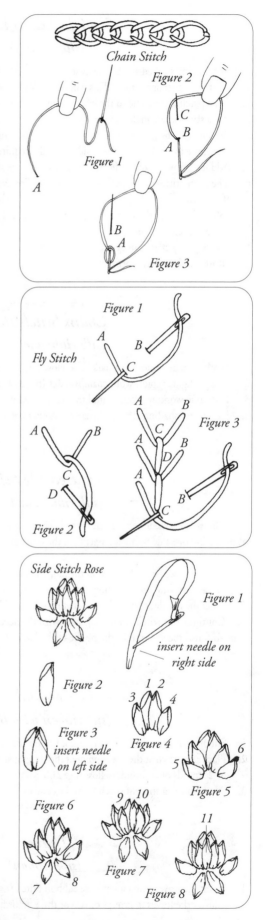

Chain Stitch
Figure 1
Figure 2
Figure 3

Fly Stitch
Figure 1
Figure 2
Figure 3

Side Stitch Rose
Figure 1
insert needle on right side
Figure 2
Figure 3
insert needle on left side
Figure 4
Figure 5
Figure 6
Figure 7
Figure 8

Straight Stitch Rose
(silk ribbon)

This is sometimes called a fish bone rose.

1. Start with a straight stitch. This will be the middle stitch of the flower (fig. 1).
2. Put a stitch at an angle to the left, crossing over the base of the middle stitch (fig. 2).
3. Put a stitch at an angle to the right, covering the base again and placing the bottom of the stitch slightly below the stitch done in step 2 (fig. 3).
4. Continue to work from side to side until the required size is achieved (fig. 4).
5. Add leaves by placing 3 shorter straight stitches at angles below the flower (fig. 5).
6. The more stitches used and the looser the tension will give greater fullness to the flower.
7. If you stop at step 3, this produces a lovely fat rosebud, especially if petal one is a dark color with a slightly lighter color for petals 2 & 3 (fig. 6). Using 7 mm ribbon for large flowers looks very nice.
8. A very pretty effect can be achieved if using 3 or 4 shades for the full rose — a little extra effort but definitely worth it.

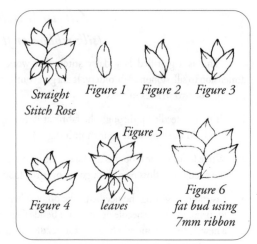

Straight Stitch Rose   Figure 1   Figure 2   Figure 3

Figure 5

Figure 4   leaves   Figure 6 fat bud using 7mm ribbon

Chain Stitch Rose
(silk ribbon or floss)

1. Work 3 French knots in a dark color close together to form a triangle (fig. 1).
2. Using a lighter color, work chain stitches (fig. 2) around the French knot (fig. 3).
3. Continue working around until the size desired is achieved (fig. 4).
4. For greater shading effects, change to another color after the first two rounds.

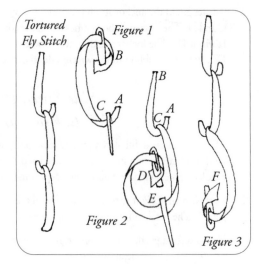

Chain Stitch Rose   Figure 1   Figure 2   Figure 3   Figure 4

Tortured Fly Stitch
(silk ribbon or floss)

This stitch is made very similar to the Fly Stitch. However, the stitches are not angled out as much and one side is much longer than the other giving the appearance of a fish hook.

1. Bring the needle to the front of the fabric at point A. Enter the needle at point B and out at C having the silk ribbon loop under the needle as it comes out at C (fig. 1).
2. Enter the needle at point D and out at E with the ribbon looped under the needle (fig. 2).
3. Continue this stitch alternating sides with the needle placement.
4. To finish the stitch, take the needle to the back of the work at F and tie off (fig. 3).

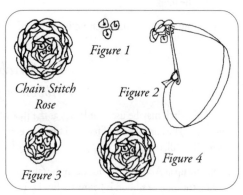

Tortured Fly Stitch   Figure 1   Figure 2   Figure 3

Rosebud
(silk ribbon with floss)

1. Stitch a straight stitch with 2mm silk ribbon (fig. 1).
2. Place a fly stitch at the lower point of the straight stitch with green DMC Flower thread or 2 strands of embroidery floss (fig. 2).
3. Work an extra straight stitch from the center of the rosebud to the base (fig. 3).

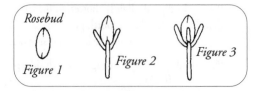

Rosebud   Figure 1   Figure 2   Figure 3

Leaves
(silk ribbon)

1. Work the leaves using a Japanese Ribbon Stitch (fig. 1).
2. Cluster the leaves in groups of two or three according to the template (fig. 2).

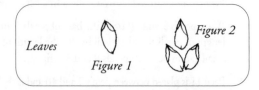

Leaves   Figure 1   Figure 2

Lady Bird
(silk ribbon with floss)

A little lady bird can look charming amongst a group of flowers.
1. Using red 4mm silk ribbon, work a ribbon stitch, piercing the silk ribbon on the right-hand side so it rolls to one side (fig. 1).
2. Work a second stitch to the right of the first stitch, piercing the ribbon on the left-hand side (fig. 2).
3. Using dark floss, work a large French knot for the head and slightly smaller ones for the body spots (fig. 3).
4. With the dark floss, work 2 pistol stitches for the antennae, and a straight stitch covering the join between the red stitches to mark the wings (fig. 4).

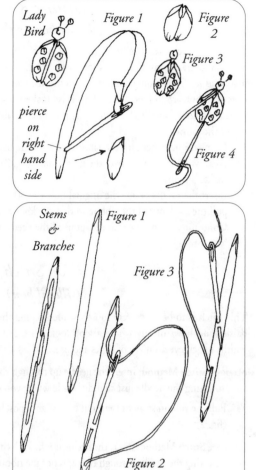

Stems and Branches
(silk ribbon and floss)

A silk ribbon and thread combination create nice flowing stems and branches for your flowers.
1. With 4mm green silk ribbon, work a ribbon stitch for the length of your stem (fig. 1).
2. When all embroidery is finished, take 2 strands of DMC floss or DMC Flower Thread and put long stitches down the center of the stems, taking a small back stitch approximately every half inch (fig. 2). Alternate from right to left as you stitch the length of the branch (fig. 3). This gives life to the stems and bridges the color jump between the sharp green of the leaves and the pale green of the stems.

Beverley Bow
(silk ribbon and floss)

This lovely bow seams to dance its way over most things I do!
1. Allow approximately 16" of silk ribbon.
2. Make two loops in the ribbon holding one loop in each hand and having an equal amount of ribbon hanging below each loop (fig. 1).
3. Wrap one loop around the other and through the center. Pull the loops into a knot (fig. 2).
4. Place the bow in the desired spot and pin into place at the center knot.
5. Using pins, flip flop the ribbon to create a pretty bow (fig. 3). Do the same with the streamers of the bow. The more twists and turns, the more life it has (fig. 4).
6. If you don't like the shape reposition the pins until the desired bow shape is created.
7. When you have created the shape you like, stitch in place with French knots, using 2 strands of embroidery thread, or D. M. C. Flower thread (fig 5).

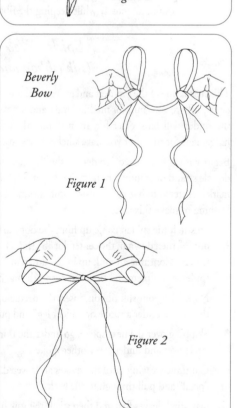

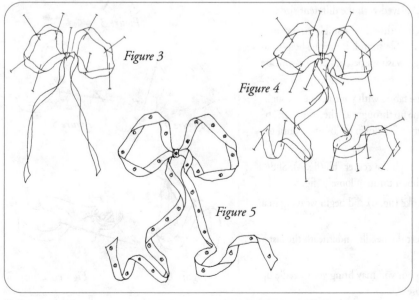

Colonial Knot
(silk ribbon or floss)

Basic knot stitches are used in a variety of ways. They can be the centers of daisies or the blossoms of hyacinths. Colonial knots make beautiful grape clusters on a vine or tiny rosettes in a bouquet. The colonial knot differs from the French knot in the method of wrapping the floss or ribbon around the needle. It will also make a larger knot than the French knot. If you want the colonial knot to be "fluffy", do not pull the ribbon tight. The knot will "sit tall" on top of the fabric.

1. Come up from beneath the fabric and wrap the needle under the ribbon one (fig. 1).
2. Next, wrap the ribbon over the needle once (fig. 2) and back under once (fig. 3). This makes a figure eight.
3. Insert the needle beside the original hole (fig. 4). While holding the needle vertically, pull the slack out of the ribbon so that the knot tightens around the needle (fig. 5). Continue holding the ribbon taut until the needle and ribbon have been pulled all the way through.

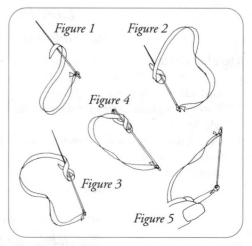

Figure 1   Figure 2

Figure 4

Figure 3

Figure 5

Loop Stitch
(silk ribbon)

This stitch is to be made very loosely while keeping the ribbon straight. It can be used for daisies and bows or any where a loop look is needed. Experiment with different ribbon widths to achieve a variety of styles and uses.

Straight Stitch Method: Insert the needle up through the fabric and loop around away from you, inserting the needle just slightly beside where you came up (fig. 1).

1. Pull the ribbon straight (without twists) and loosely adjust the loop to the desired size (fig. 2).

Japanese Stitch Method: Insert the needle up through the fabric and this time loop it towards you, inserting the needle through the center of the ribbon just beside where the needle came up (fig. 3). Again, pull loosely while keeping the ribbon straight.

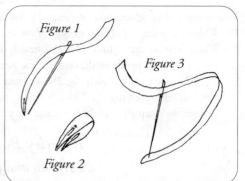

Figure 1

Figure 3

Figure 2

Spider Web Rose
(silk ribbon and floss)

This rose is one of the prettiest and easiest of all the silk ribbon stitched roses. Use 13mm for large puffy roses, 7mm for medium roses and 4mm for small roses. The spokes or "legs" on the spider will be shorter for 4mm ribbon than for 7mm ribbon. You will gain a good judgement for this after you have stitches a few roses and played with the different sizes.

Begin with a five legged "spider, or five spokes, stitched with either a single strand or a double strand of embroidery floss. For larger roses use a double strand. It may be helpful to mark a center with five evenly spaced dots around it using a washout pen or pencil as you are learning to make this rose.

1. To stitch the spider, come up from the bottom of the fabric with your needle through dot "a" then down in the center dot "b" (fig. 1). Come up through "c" then down in "b" (fig. 2). Continue around; up in "d" down in "b", up in "e" down in "b" etc... until the spider is complete and tie off underneath (fig. 3).

2. Now, with your silk ribbon, insert the needle up through the center "b" (fig. 4). Slide the needle under a spoke or "spider leg" and pull ribbon through loosely (fig. 5).

3. Skipping over the next spoke, go under the third spoke (fig. 6) and begin weaving in a circle over and under every other spoke (fig. 7).

4. Continue weaving until the spokes are covered. Insert the needle underneath the last "petal" and pull through to the back.

You may stitch leaves first and then stitch the rose on top, or you may bring your needle up from underneath a "petal" and stitch leaves under the rose.

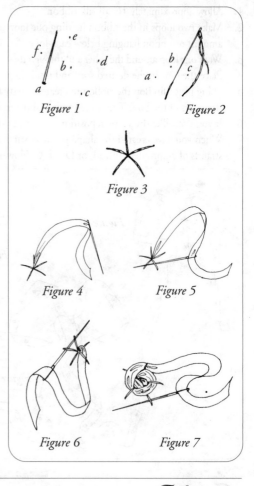

Figure 1   Figure 2

Figure 3

Figure 4

Figure 5

Figure 6

Figure 7